BANGERTER'S INVENTIONS

===HIS===

MARVELOUS

TIME CLOCK

EDITED BY KING

British Library Cataloguing-in-Publication Data
A catalogue record for this book is available from the
British Library

A History of Clocks and Watches

Horology (from the Latin, Horologium) is the science of measuring time. Clocks, watches, clockwork, sundials, clepsydras, timers, time recorders, marine chronometers and atomic clocks are all examples of instruments used to measure time. In current usage, horology refers mainly to the study of mechanical time-keeping devices, whilst chronometry more broadly included electronic devices that have largely supplanted mechanical clocks for accuracy and precision in time-keeping. Horology itself has an incredibly long history and there are many museums and several specialised libraries devoted to the subject. Perhaps the most famous is the *Royal Greenwich Observatory*, also the source of the Prime Meridian (longitude 0° 0' 0"), and the home of the first marine timekeepers accurate enough to determine longitude.

The word 'clock' is derived from the Celtic words *clagan* and *clocca* meaning 'bell'. A silent instrument missing such a mechanism has traditionally been known as a timepiece, although today the words have become interchangeable. The clock is one of the oldest human interventions, meeting the need to consistently measure intervals of time shorter than the natural units: the day, the lunar month and the year. The current sexagesimal system of time measurement dates to approximately 2000 BC in Sumer. The Ancient Egyptians divided the day into two twelve-hour periods and used large obelisks to track the movement of the sun. They also developed water clocks, which had also been employed frequently by the Ancient Greeks, who called them 'clepsydrae'. The Shang Dynasty is also believed to have used the outflow water clock around the same time.

The first mechanical clocks, employing the verge escapement mechanism (the mechanism that controls the rate of a clock by advancing the gear train at regular intervals or 'ticks') with a foliot or balance wheel timekeeper (a weighted wheel that rotates back and forth, being returned toward its centre position by a spiral), were invented in Europe at around the start of the fourteenth century. They became the standard timekeeping device until the pendulum clock was invented in 1656. This remained the most accurate timekeeper until the 1930s, when quartz oscillators (where the mechanical **resonance** of a vibrating crystal is used to create an electrical signal with a very precise **frequency**) were invented, followed by atomic clocks after World War Two. Although initially limited to laboratories, the development of microelectronics in the 1960s made **quartz clocks** both compact and cheap to produce, and by the 1980s they became the world's dominant timekeeping technology in both clocks and **wristwatches**.

The concept of the wristwatch goes back to the production of the very earliest watches in the sixteenth century. Elizabeth I of England received a wristwatch from Robert Dudley in 1571, described as an arm watch. From the beginning, they were almost exclusively worn by women, while men used pocket-watches up until the early twentieth century. This was not just a matter of fashion or prejudice; watches of the time were notoriously prone to fouling from exposure to the elements, and could only reliably be kept safe from harm if carried securely in the pocket. Wristwatches were first worn by military men towards the end of the nineteenth century, when the importance of synchronizing manoeuvres during war without potentially revealing the plan to the enemy through signalling was increasingly recognized. It was clear that using pocket watches while in the heat of battle or while mounted on a horse was impractical, so officers began to strap the watches to their wrist.

The company H. Williamson Ltd., based in Coventry, England, was one of the first to capitalize on this opportunity. During the company's 1916 AGM it was noted that '...the public is buying the practical things of life. Nobody can truthfully contend that the watch is a luxury. It is said that one soldier in every four wears a wristlet watch, and the other three mean to get one as soon as they can.' By the end of the War, almost all enlisted men wore a wristwatch, and after they were demobilized, the fashion soon caught on - the British *Horological Journal* wrote in 1917 that '...the wristlet watch was little used by the sterner sex before the war, but now is seen on the wrist of nearly every man in uniform and of many men in civilian attire.' Within a decade, sales of wristwatches had outstripped those of pocket watches.

Now that clocks and watches had become 'common objects' there was a massively increased demand on clockmakers for maintenance and repair. Julien Le Roy, a clockmaker of Versailles, invented a face that could be opened to view the inside clockwork – a development which many subsequent artisans copied. He also invented special repeating mechanisms to improve the precision of clocks and supervised over 3,500 watches. The more complicated the device however, the more often it needed repairing. Today, since almost all clocks are now factory-made, most modern clockmakers *only* repair clocks. They are frequently employed by jewellers, antique shops or places devoted strictly to repairing clocks and watches.

The clockmakers of the present must be able to read blueprints and instructions for numerous types of clocks and time pieces that vary from antique clocks to modern time pieces in order to fix and make clocks or watches. The trade requires fine motor coordination as clockmakers must frequently work on devices with small gears and fine machinery, as well as an appreciation for the original art form. As is evident from this very short history of clocks and watches, over the centuries the items themselves have changed – almost out of recognition, but the importance of time-keeping has not. It is an area which provides a constant source of fascination and scientific discovery, still very much evolving today. We hope the reader enjoys this book.

CONTENTS

DREAM OF AGES REALIZED

THE Twentieth Century is the century of successful accomplishment. The zenith of human achievements appears to have been reached. Yet every day brings its new surprises. There seems to be no limit to the output of human genius and ingenuity. We have now the aeroplane skimming through the air with bird-like ease and rapidity; the wireless telegraph and wireless telephone; the leviathan steamship "Olympic," which annihilates distance between Europe and America and a sight of which would make our ancestors gasp in amazement, as well as other modern marvels.

And these pages tell about one of the greatest inventions of all time—a discovery of to-day that will add a crowning glory to successful Twentieth Century endeavor.

Bangerter's Perpetulium Time Clock is most concrete, tangible and eloquent evidence that PERPETUAL FORCE—the greatest of all mechanical problems—is solved at last.

PERPETUAL FORCE!

Bangerter's latest and highly successful creation sounds like a fairy story realized. The wizardry of true genius is thus marvellously expressed. Volumes have been written by prominent authors and leading scientific men illustrating the wasted efforts and picturing the despair of many inventors in all ages who failed in their persistent efforts to solve the problem of perpetual force—producing motion. Centuries of unwearying studies and activities only met with failure. It was called an impossible task, a phantom, a phantasy, a freak of the imagination that never could be converted to a practical issue.

But the failure of those who attempted and failed in the past could not keep back the energy and force of progress.

To-day the problem of perpetual force is really solved. It remained for a young Swiss inventor—Mr. Friedrich Bangerter—to successfully accomplish the heretofore impossible.

Bangerter's Perpetual Time Clock is perfect in theory and practice. It is operated by a principle that cannot fail. A glance at the machine will convince the most skeptical.

From time to time we read of wonderful inventions that never get beyond the stage where they are talked about. They are impractical and impossible, because their inventors are fakirs, fanatics or dreamers—inventors lacking the character, knowledge and brains to understand whether or not their ideas are of any realizable value.

A PRACTICAL INVENTION

This is emphatically not the case with Mr. Bangerter. His is a most practical mind. His record as an inventor is one of successes. He has had twenty years' experience as a practical and technical mechanical engineer, with a great number of patents and inventions in operation all over the world. His marvelous automatic machines—taking wrought casting and bars of metal and automatically making gears, chains, spindles, screws, pinions, etc., of the highest precision—is a striking example of his great ability.

At two World's Expositions—in Paris, 1900, and Belgium, 1905—the Jury of International Selection of Mechanical Experts awarded him Silver and Gold Medals and Diplomas for his inventions of the most marvelous machines.

A TRULY WONDERFUL INVENTION

Bangerter's Perpetual Time Clock is a truly wonderful mechanism and an exact, reliable timepiece. It will do the work for which it is intended, as long as the mechanical parts hold together—as long as the shafts and spindles run in their bearings.

In other words, this clock will run for generations—

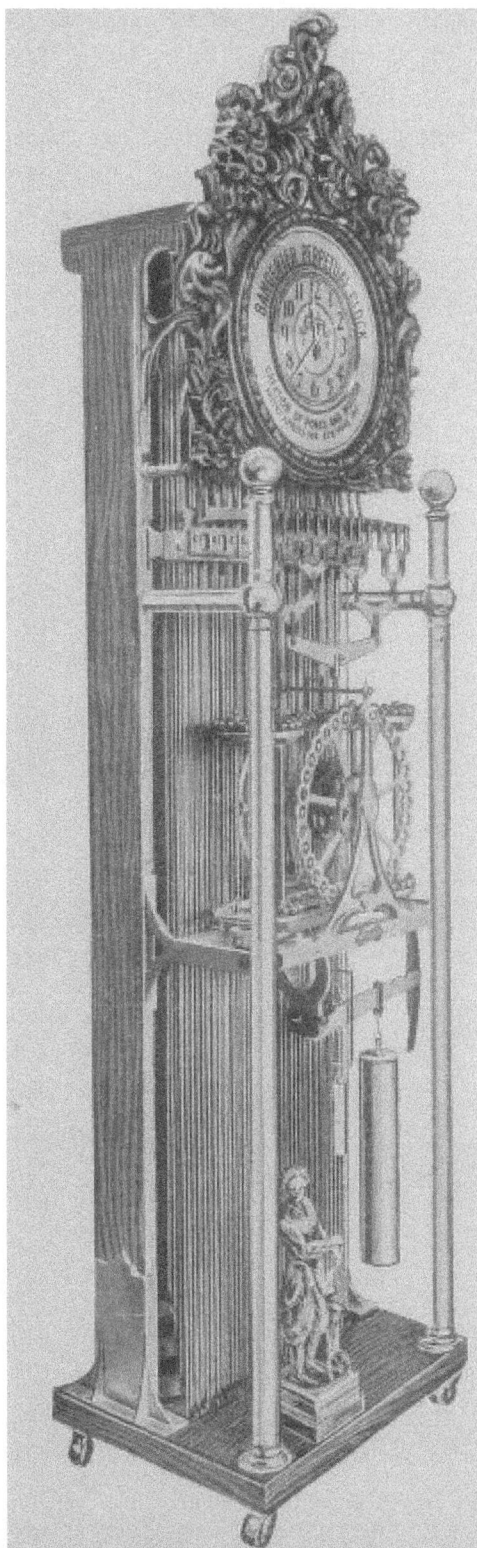

BANGERTER'S
PERPETUAL
CLOCK.

yes, from 100 to 500 years—without winding. During this unbelievably long period this clock will run, show the exact time, strike the hours and play the marvelous Westminster melodies without the slightest expenditure of time or effort in winding up with springs or weights.

There is employed no electricity, chemicals, secret preparations or fuel, to produce the power and energy to run Bangerter's Perpetual Force Clock. Yet there is a natural law behind it all—the secret of its practical application was discovered and successfully applied by the young Swiss inventor.

WHAT DOES PERPETUAL MOTION MEAN?

To avoid loss of time and to obviate dissension and discussion between readers and critics herewith is given the technical understanding of the title "PERPETUAL MOTION." It is taken from "The International Cyclopedia," Vol. II, Page 522, and reads as follows:

"Perpetual Motion means an engine which, without any supply of power from without, can not only maintain its own motion forever, or as long as its material lasts, but can also be applied to drive machinery, and therefore to do external work. In other words, it means a device for creating power energy without corresponding expenditure. This is now known to be absolutely impossible, no matter what physical forces be employed."

The Bangerter Clock is eloquent evidence that the theory just quoted (and heretofore generally accepted as correct) is not, in fact, correct. It will be necessary, in the face of this new discovery, to write a new definition of Perpetual Motion.

Impossibilities of yesterday are the stern realities of to-day. We have now arrived at such a stage of advancement as to be surprised at no discovery or invention, no matter how improbable or wonderful.

NAPOLEON'S FATAL ERROR.

Napoleon was advised not to listen to Fulton's plan of the steamboat—a certain cause of his downfall,for had he accepted Fulton's radical and previously unheard of ideas he would presently have a fleet of steamships.

He would thus be Emperor of the Ocean, for with his fleet of steamships he would surely have conquered Britain's old-fashioned sailing navy.

Ten years ago all the scientific men to whom Bangerter presented his plans for an airship, gravely shook their heads. They said:—

"Your principle is right—it shows the most practical device we have yet seen, and if there were such proposition as a 'heavier-than-air' possibility you would have the best chance of success."

Very well, the "heavier-than-air" possibility has become a certainty. To-day scientific men see the weight of a man's body (increased by a heavy framework and many mechanical contrivances) soar lightly and majestically between the blue sky and the earth below. The dream of the pitied and sneered at inventor of a decade ago is exemplified to-day all over the civilized world!

All this the scientists a few years ago did not see.

The new born force—insignificant in size and appearance, but giant-like in actual force—now known as the gasolene engine, did not then make an appearance. But now hundreds of machines are flying all over the world —propelled by the pygmy gasolene engine.

In other words, as the force of a man is mechanically figured to 1-7 of one H. P., some gasolene engines of the weight and size of a man develop 700 times more power.

This enormous force may soon bring about a revolution in warfare by displacing powder as a force to expel bullets from guns.

Tests made last year with a small model gun have demonstrated great possibilities by shooting small 3-8 inch round ball-bearing at so terrific a speed that they pierced a 1½-inch pine target at 60 feet distance, and in such enormous quantities that inside of a few seconds five targets were riddled to atoms.

FLYING MACHINES EVERYWHERE.

Aeroplanes are to-day counted by hundreds. Some carry ten or more men at a time, and keeping it up for hours with a speed of nearly 100 miles per hour.

How great is the number of the wonderful time-saving, effort-saving and distance-annihilating inventions of the past fifty years!

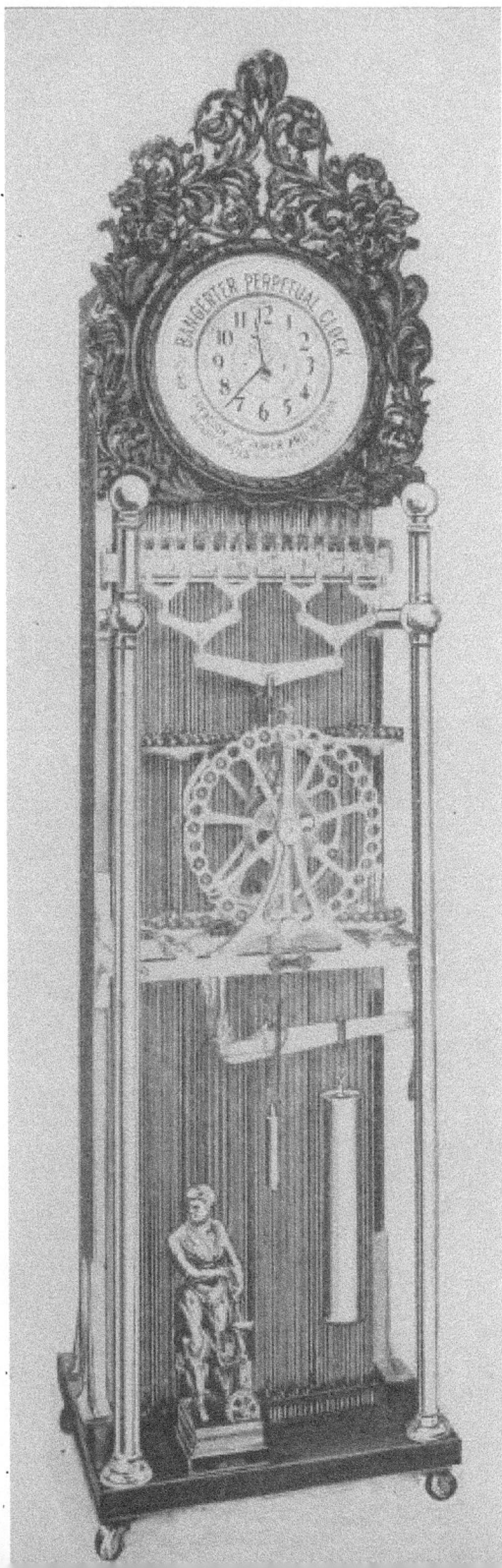

BANGERTER'S
PERPETUAL
CLOCK.

How wonderful is the transformation! How sudden and how amazingly great is the progress that a single generation produces in this remarkable century! Great men have lived before us. Intellectual giants were our fathers and grandfathers. But the time had not come for the infinite hand to touch the mainspring that would set all these fountains of activity to pouring out their rich treasures of knowledge and invention. But as soon as the time is reached, how supremely marvelous are the undreamed-of achievements!

AMERICA! LAND OF OPPORTUNITIES.

The development of the greatest of all countries—the United States of America—is a most prolific source and cause of inventions. After the Civil War had proven that equality and freedom were not mere figures of speech, but that they were real, substantial blessings to be enjoyed by all American citizens, a great stimulus to inventive genius was given. The brains responded to the call for improvement and development.

The winnings from mining, the rewards from manufacture, the profits to be derived in the thousand and one forms of commerce and the handsome payments to be derived from agriculture, lumbering, cattle raising, fruit culture, etc., were the strongest possible incentives to the exercise of brains and inventive ingenuity.

Manufacture and commerce were fostered and developed by rapid transportation. Railroads and steamships soon ran wherever needed. Prosperity and happiness were the natural results of this wholesale national activity.

The machinery of warfare, such as marine fortifications, great guns and war vessels, was installed and maintained at an enormous expense.

It is not too much to say that America's prosperity has aroused the greatest possible interest in European countries. They have made the most strenuous exertions in order to compete in the world's trade marts.

STIMULUS TO INVENTIVE GENIUS.

A long period of universal peace has made it possible to keep up inventive investigation and experimenting with marvelously fruitful results.

Up to the present time more than ONE MILLION PATENTS have been issued for the United States alone. Truly a marvelous record!

PERPETUAL MOTION—THE STUDY OF AGES.

In every age inventors have dreamed of that problem of problems—Perpetual Motion. It is a problem that has exhausted the mind, purse and patience of thousands of inventors. Almost every one has heard of some one else's interest in this great subject. But history shows that the study of perpetual motion has been tinctured with charlatanism.

Fakirs have from time to time shown contrivances which seemed to solve the problem, but were delusions and humbugs pure and simple, as they were gotten up to delude the public and deceive investors. The notorious Keely Motor was but one case of many.

Notwithstanding the enormous amount of unsuccessful effort and study in an endeavor to solve Perpetual Motion there are yet many enthusiastic students earnestly laboring in the field.

There is one great Perpetual Motion. It is Nature's own handiwork, and the only successful human attempt is exemplified in Bangerter's marvelously combined clockwork in which the silent forces of Nature are harnessed to carry out immutable laws. Similar attempts had already been undertaken by scientific men, but without success, until Friedrich Bangerter touched the true keynote.

WHEN NATURE IS READY.

The time and conditions were ripe and ready. So was the man! It seems to be one of the great laws of Mother Nature to withhold her most precious secrets until she sees fit to divulge them, and then she brings in happy juxtaposition "The Time, The Place and The Man."

This has proven true with most of the world's most important inventions and discoveries. Nature in her own good time gives up the priceless secret—that little something that spells success and that was so long sought after until the golden moment it was revealed.

BANGERTER'S
PERPETUAL
CLOCK.

Had Lilienthal to-day's gasolene engine—an engine developing 100 H. P. to the weight of only 200 pounds, as the rotary Gnome Engine, he would have been highly successful in his efforts to fly.

The development of the automobile meant the development of the gasolene engine, which became so reduced in weight and so powerful in action that all that was necessary was to attach it to some planes, revolve propellers, and, presto! off went the flying machine with ease and speed.

As time goes on and as the needs of men multiply other great inventions will be perfected in obedience to the universal Law of Creation.

Every student of Perpetual Motion, yes, every intelligent observer of the world's progress, will be intensely interested in Bangerter's wonderful clock.

OTHER NATURAL FORCES.

There are many other natural sources that could be called in to develop Perpetual Force for clocks, machinery, etc., just as waterfalls, rainfalls, the blowing of winds, etc., but all these could not be considered and compared with Bangerter's inventions. They are at present impractical on account of the extensive and expensive outside connections required.

Streams are sometimes found only at great distances, and the entire system of turbines, dynamos, electrical conducting wires and motors are much too complicated to operate a simple system of your own.

VARIATION OF TEMPERATURE.

We cannot depend upon a wind or a rainfall, but we can always depend upon a variation of temperature day after day and year after year. Some days there may be a variation of only one or two degrees, other days from 15 to 25 degrees, but no matter what the variation may be, Bangerter's machine collects the daily results and stores their energies.

These results are produced day after day by the phenomena of expansion and contraction of material, and is so combined as to always have sufficient force stored to always keep the clock running.

In other words, Bangerter's Perpetulium Time Clock will always run without winding.

Even if there should be no variation of temperature for a period of several days or weeks—which will never happen as long as the world exists—sufficient force would be stored from past variations to keep it running for a considerable period of time.

This clock will give perfect time in any room, in any house or building and in any exterior or interior location. It is not affected by time or locality. The mysterious forces of Nature operate it equally as well in the jungles of Africa as in a New York or London mansion.

It is the one clock for all time, all localities and all conditions.

NATURE'S MANY PHENOMENA.

How marvelous and manifold are the workings of Nature! Her phenomena and secrets are ever subjects of intense study by the world's greatest intellects.

Nature's manifestations are mild, majestic, mighty, cold, calm, bounteous, benign, beneficent, beautiful, terrific, tender, temperate—in fact, every adjective in the English language could be employed to describe her full gamut of moods.

Some of us have heard the furious roaring of a blizzard and observed the enormous force and terrific speed of the tempest, leaving behind death and destruction in its wake. Many towns, large and small, have been swept out of existence by blizzards, tornadoes and cyclones.

And the silent, fructifying forces of Nature—how grand and beautiful beyond expression do they accomplish their work! "Great oaks from little acorns grow," and from little, apparently insignificant seeds spring monarch trees of the forest, their crowns majestically waving three and four hundred feet in the air. The mysteries of life have yet been revealed to no man, and the artist has not lived who has been able to paint the picture, to catch the true color effects, that only Mother Nature can depict on a world wide canvas.

NATURE'S GREAT PLANETARY CLOCKWORK.

Every atom of force in the universe performs a purpose and function. Nature never makes a mistake.

BANGERTER'S
PERPETUAL
CLOCK.

Each of the myriad forces under her control has the most logical cause for existence, and all are under the guidance of the most perfect system. The entire planetary system may be termed the Clockwork of the Universe—the great Natural Clock, absolutely authoritative and perfect in operation and giving us days, nights, seasons and variations of temperature with a regularity that never fails. .

These variations of temperature really mean the source of all life and vegetation. In order that we human beings live the globe must revolve on its axis, and as the year grows on apace we receive the heat rays from another planet—the Sun—in different angles and positions and in the variations of temperature ranging from extreme heat to extreme cold.

HEAT THE SOURCE OF ALL POWER.

From heat comes all power. When the latent forces of Nature were first set aflame by primitive man he touched the spring of civilization. Since that time fire has been working for human progress. It is one of the most powerful agents in the development of civilization.

Our rude ancestors long ago discovered its great utility, and they cudgeled their brains to aid the flame of fire and obtain a still fiercer heat. The bellows was the result—the wind pointed the way to this invention.

Then followed by slow degrees the acquirement of further knowledge concerning fire and its uses. Our forefathers learned the processes of melting and smelting —later were established various metallurgical operations.

The path was thus prepared for Tubal Cain and other artificers in metals. Man eventually became exceedingly skilled in applying heat forces in his many requirements in articles of brass, tin, zinc, steel, etc.

HEAT—EXPANSION AND CONTRACTION.

From an article by J. Gordon Ogden, Ph.D., in "Popular Mechanics," September, 1910, we quote:

"Expansion is one of the most remarkable of the phenomena to be reckoned with in the natural world.

Practically every bit of matter from the Great Brooklyn Bridge to the tiny hairspring in one's watch is under its imperial domination. It is a tremendous force, and the world of mechanics has to treat it with the deference and respect due to its gigantic power. Unlike gravity, and other forces of nature, it is whimsical and takes sudden fits and starts, now acting one way, now another. It affects different bodies in different ways, and seems to be at variance with the time-honored forces whose action can be predicted under all circumstances. At least that is what it apparently does. In our meagre knowledge of the great underlying laws that control the universe it is possibly unwise to speak so unkindly of expansion, as though it were a spoiled child in need of correction; its behavior, however, is so contrary to what one might expect that one is at a loss to say anything else.

"The walls of a building are sometimes rectified by the enormous force exerted by the contraction of iron rods. Bars of iron are placed so as to join the two walls where the bulging is most pronounced. These bars terminate in screws furnished with nuts. The whole of their length is heated and the nuts tightened. On cooling the bars will contract with practically irresistible force, causing the walls to straighten up. This operation is repeated until the rectification is completed. Boiler plates are fastened with red-hot rivets. The contraction of the rivets incident upon their cooling draws the plates tightly together, forming a steam-proof joint."

"Tyndall, in his work on heat, gives an excellent illustration of the force of expansion and contraction. 'The choir of Bristol Cathedral was covered with sheet lead, the length of the covering being 60 feet and its depth 19 feet 5 inches. It had been laid in the year 1851, and two years afterward it had moved bodily down for a distance of 18 inches. The descent had been continually going on from the time the lead had been laid down, and an attempt to stop it by driving nails into the rafters had failed, for the force with which the lead had descended was sufficient to draw out the nails. The roof was not a steep one, and the lead could have rested on it forever without sliding down by gravity. What, then, was the cause of the descent? The lead was exposed to the varying temperatures of day and night. During the day the heat imparted to it caused it to expand. Had it lain upon a horizontal surface, it would have expanded all around; but as it lay upon an inclined surface it expanded more freely downward than upward. When, on the contrary, the lead contracted at night its upper edge was drawn more easily downward than its lower edge upward. Its motion was, therefore, exactly like that of a common earthworm; it pushed its lower edge forward during the day and drew its upper edge after it during the night, and thus by degrees it crawled through a space of 18 inches in two years.'

"Mention has been made in a preceding article of the effect of unequal expansion upon two different metals that have been bolted together. It is by this principle that the action of the ordinary thermostat, so familiar now as a controller and regulator of the temperature of high buildings, is explained—a rod made up of two different metals whose rates of expansion are different. When the temperature of the room in which the thermostat is placed becomes too high the rod curls toward the metal point S and touches it, completing an electrical contact which causes a motor to shut off the draft. When the temperature of the room falls below a certain point the rod curls in the opposite direction toward the metal point T. This causes a motor to open the draft and thus furnish a more abundant supply of hot air.

"Everybody in these days of cheap and reliable time-pieces carries a watch. And yet there are very few who appreciate the methods and devices by means of which the troublesome expansion and contraction of metals are corrected, in order that a watch may keep correct time. The balance wheel of a watch corresponds to the pendulum of a clock, and any variation in its dimensions will cause it to move faster or slower, as the case may be. The hairspring is really a long strip of metal which becomes weakened in its effect when expanded by an increase in temperature and has its power augmented when contraction takes place.

"To correct both of these conditions the rim of the balance wheel is made up of two different metals, the outer part brass, the inner part iron. When the hairspring becomes weaker by expansion the brass of the balance wheel also expands; but as it expands more than the iron to which it is bonded, it curls in toward the center of the wheel, making practically a wheel of smaller diameter, and causing the same effect as is produced when a clock pendulum is shortened. Exactly the opposite conditions obtain when the timepiece is exposed to extreme cold and the balance wheel has its diameter increased, thus causing a slowing up to counteract the increased strain produced by the contraction of the hairspring. The same principle is applied in the construction of first-class clocks. Any uncorrected variation in the length of a pendulum is fatal to the timekeeping quality of a clock. A gridiron pendulum made up of alternate rods of steel and brass serves to correct the result of the expansive force.

"The central steel rod passes through holes in the lower horizontal framework and supports the bob at the lower end. The steel rods are so arranged that they will expand downward, while the brass rods expand upward and the total length of each metal used is exactly sufficient to counteract each other's expansion, and the centre of the bob will remain at a constant distance from the point of suspension."

Scientific men and engineers are more or less familiar with the phenomena of expansion. But no inventor produced a system capable of utilizing this force to run a clock until Bangerter succeeded in mastering the problem.

Bangerter's clock is unquestionably a triumph of human ingenuity. It is a mechanical masterpiece. Herewith follows the complete specification:

SPECIFICATION

TO ALL WHOM IT MAY CONCERN:

Be it known that I, FRIEDRICH BANGERTER, of the City of New York (Borough of Richmond), County of Richmond and State of New York, have invented certain new and useful improvements in

APPARATUS FOR THE EDUCTION, STORAGE AND APPLICATION OF ENERGY FROM EXPANSIBLE MATERIALS,

of which the following is a full, clear and exact specification, such as will enable others skilled in the art to which it appertains to make and use the same.

This invention relates to apparatus whereby energy may be educed from expansible materials, due to the expansion and contraction thereof on changes of temperature, and the said energy either applied direct or stored and applied for the purpose of operating machines and devices of various kinds.

I show and describe herein two forms of apparatus for obtaining such expansion and contraction and the required energy therefrom, and I also show two forms in which the energy so obtained is accumulated and stored. In connection therewith, I show the application of my invention to the running of clocks, but it will be understood that the invention is not limited in its application to that particular class of machine, and that it may be applied to any use of which it is susceptible.

It is well known that all metals are capable of some degree of expansion and contraction, and some metals have this property in greater degree than others. The amount of expansion for each degree rise in temperature is quite regular, and is called the co-efficient of expansion. It is also well known that zinc has this property in greater degree than any other of the solid metals, its co-efficient of linear expansion being appreciably higher. For this reason, as well as because of its relatively low cost, I preferably make use of zinc in the construction of the expansible parts of my apparatus.

One of the objects of my invention, therefore, is to provide an expansion device of novel construction and arrangement, which will generate energy and maintain motion during changes in temperature, to such an appreciable and useful amount, as to constitute it in fact a temperature motor.

A further object of my invention is to provide means for accumulating or storing the energy thus generated.

A further object is to provide means for applying the energy thus generated and stored.

Other objects, such as compactness, durability and comparatively low cost of the apparatus, will appear in the following description, in which reference is had to the accompanying drawings.

In the drawings:—

Fig. 1 is a front elevation, showing the application of my invention to a clock provided, in this case, with a mainspring as usual;

Fig. 2 is a rear elevation of the same with a part removed;

Fig. 3 is an enlarged perspective detail showing how the strips forming part of the expansion member or coil are connected up;

Fig. 4 is a sectional view, on lines 5—5 of Fig. 1;

Fig. 5 is an enlarged detail elevation, with parts removed;

Fig. 6 is an enlarged detail cross section of the central portion of the apparatus, with part broken away;

Fig. 7 is a rear elevation of the same with parts broken away;

Fig. 8 is an enlarged detail of the upper portion of the apparatus shown in Fig. 4, with parts removed;

Fig. 9 is a perspective detail, partly broken away;

Fig. 10 is an enlarged detail of a portion of the ratchet mechanism shown in the lower portion of Figs. 6 and 7;

Fig. 11 is an enlarged section of a flexible coupling shown in Fig. 7;

Fig. 12 is an elevation of a modification of the expansion coil;

Fig. 12[a] is a perspective view showing how two of such modified expansion coils may be connected;

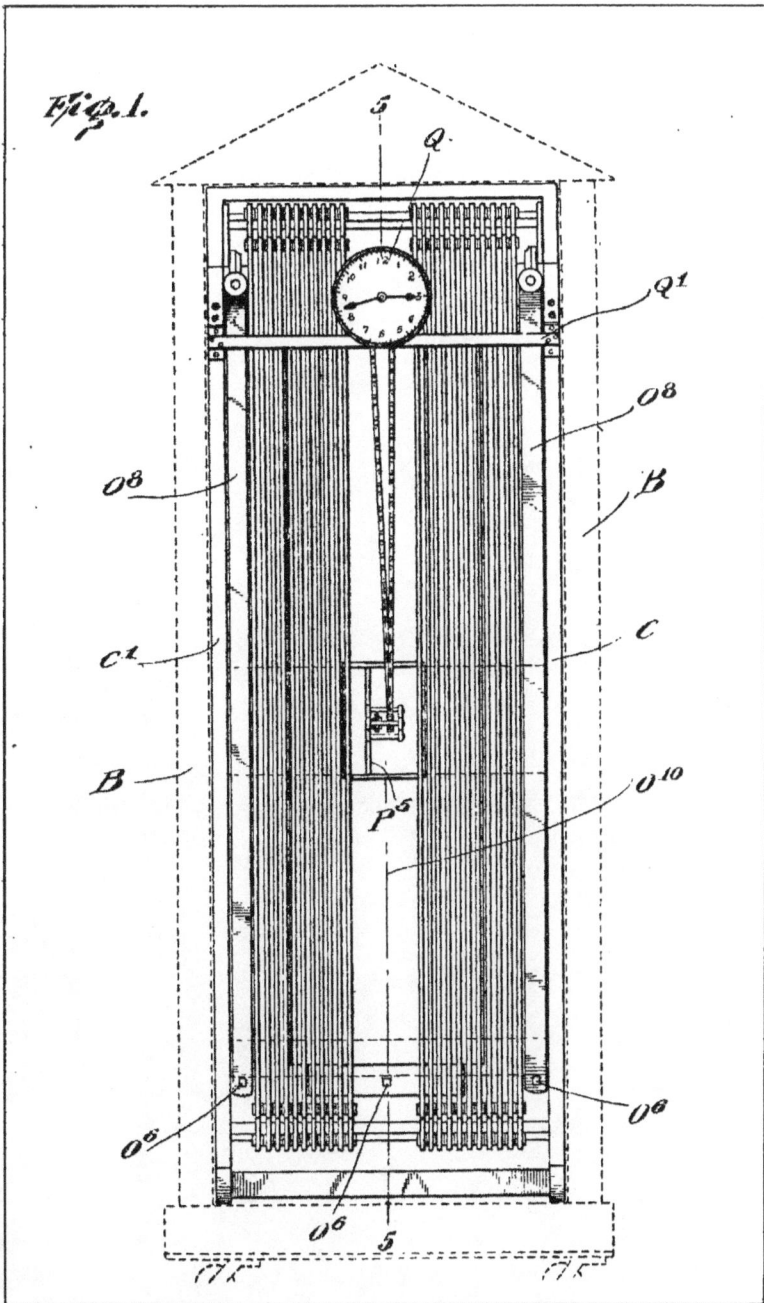

Fig. 1.

BANGERTER'S PERPETUAL TIME CLOCK

Fig. 13 is a front elevation showing my invention applied to another form of force storage mechanism;

Fig. 14 is a plan view of same, on lines 14—14 of Fig. 13;

Fig. 15 is a rear elevation on lines 15—15 of Fig. 14;

Fig. 16 is a vertical section on lines 16—16 of Fig. 14;

Fig. 17 is an enlarged detail of part of the apparatus shown in the upper portion of Fig. 16;

Fig. 18 is an enlarged detail of the ball-discharging means shown in the lower portion of Fig. 16;

Fig. 19 is an enlarged detail of the loading device shown in the opposite part of the lower portion of Fig. 16; and

Fig. 20 is a plan view on lines 20—20 of Fig. 13.

Referring to the construction illustrated in Fig. 1 to 11, inclusive, B represents the outer frame of the apparatus.

Mounted within the outer frame B is an inner frame comprising the uprights C, C^1, which are rigidly secured by cross-bars D^1, D^2.

The outer frame B, as well as the inner frame uprights C, C^1 are preferably formed of wood or other material capable of a low degree of expansion.

Within the upper and lower ends of the inner frame are anti-friction knife-bars E, E^1, the upper one of which, E, has each end within a vertically disposed slot E^2 in the uprights C, C^1, within which said knife-bar may be moved vertically, as hereinafter described.

Each end of the lower knife-bar E^1 lies immovable within a recess in a plate E^3 mounted on each of the uprights C, C^1.

These knife-bars, which are preferably formed of hardened steel, have oppositely disposed relatively sharp edges E^5, which act as bearings for a series of horizontally disposed anti-friction levers, F, F^1, which I will term balance-levers, since they are intended to balance evenly and freely on the thin edges of the knife-bars with little friction somewhat in the nature of a scale-balance. These levers are pivotally connected to a series of metallic expansion strips G, G^1, G^2, G^3, etc., the construction and arrangement and manner of connecting up the same being more clearly shown in Fig. 3.

It will be observed that the arrangement of the levers F and expansion strips G, G^1, etc., is such as to form, in effect, a spiral, the short strip G being connected to one end of one of the balance-levers F, and the strip G being connected at its lower end to the opposite end of said lever, the upper end of said strip G^1 being connected to one end of the first one of the levers F^1. To the opposite end of said lever F^1 the upper end of strip G^2 is connected, the lower end of said strip being connected to the left-hand end of the second one of the levers F, and so on to the final short strip G^x. The levers F, F^1 must be formed of a metal capable of withstanding great strain without bending, and for this purpose I prefer to use the metal known as macadamite.

For convenience of designation, I will refer to each of these groups of balance-levers F, F^1, and expansion strips G, G^1, etc., as expansion coils, and while I have herein shown but two sets of such expansion coils, it is to be understood that there may be any number of such sets desired, and any desired number of strips and levers composing such coils, depending upon the character of the work to be performed.

Furthermore, I desire it to be understood that when I use the terms "strips"—as characterizing the members connecting the balance levers—either in the specification or claims, I do not limit myself to the form of connecting member or "strips" shown, but mean to include in the use of the term "strips" any other form such as wires, rods or bars of either square, round, hexagonal or other cross sectional shape.

The ends of the short strips G, G^x are connected by wires H, H^1 with the opposite ends of what I will term a coil lever I, which, as more clearly shown in Fig. 5, is keyed to a shaft J, which latter has its end journaled upon the cross-bars J^1, J^2 secured to the uprights C, C^1 of the inner frame of the apparatus, and this shaft I will name a coil shaft.

Keyed to the coil shaft J is a lever K, which it may be proper to designate as a stress lever, since from it is suspended a weight K^1, the function of which is to place a certain amount of stress upon the series of expansion strips and balance-levers composing the expansion coil, keeping the metal of the strips slightly stretched and preventing any loss of motion at the different points of connection, and thereby furthering a very important object, which is to make of each series of expansion strips

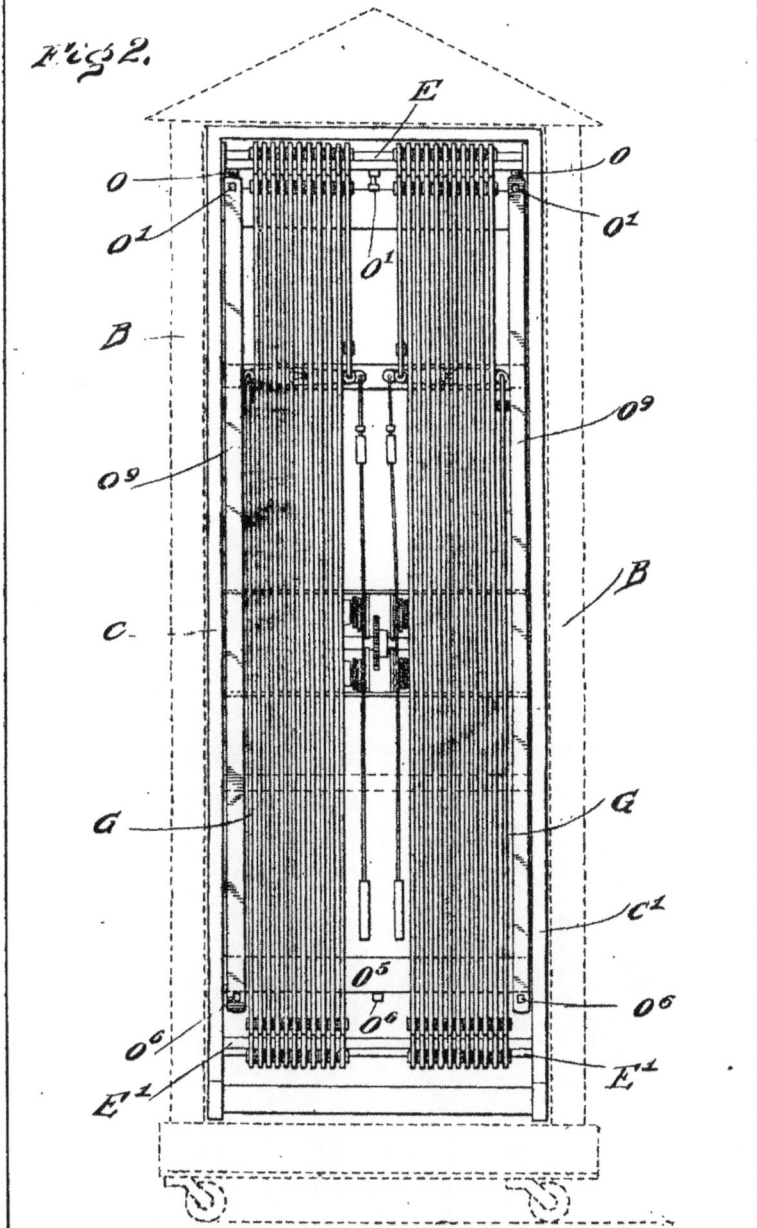

BANGERTER'S PERPETUAL TIME CLOCK

and balance-levers a single spiral unit, throughout which the expansion and contraction of the strips are transmitted.

Also keyed to the shaft J is a power transmisson lever L, and any rotary motion imparted to said shaft is necessarily imparted to the lever L in the form of reciprocating motion.

Referring now to the power storage device, one or a number of which may be used in connection with my expansion coils.

Disposed approximately midway of the uprights C, C^1 and within casing M, secured at its ends to said uprights, is rotatably mounted a power transmission shaft M^1, keyed to which is a spur wheel M^2. Also mounted on the shaft M^1 is a spur wheel M^3, meshing with which at its upper and lower sides are two spur wheels M^4, M^5, loosely mounted upon short supporting shafts M^6, M^7, journaled in uprights M^8, M^8 secured to the casing M. To each of the spur wheels M^4, M^5 is secured the outer end of a coil spring M^9, M^{10}, respectively, the inner ends of said springs being secured to the respective shafts M^6, M^7, the arrangement being such that when the springs are placed under tension by the rotation of the shafts M^6, M^7, the force of the springs rotates the spur wheels M^4, M^5, thereby rotating the spur wheel M^3, shaft M^1 and the spur wheel M^2.

Also mounted upon each of the respective short shafts M^6, M^7, and keyed thereto, is a ratchet wheel M^{11}, M^{12}, and adjacent thereto and loosely mounted upon each of said shafts M^6, M^7 is a pawl carrier plate M^{13}, M^{14}, each carrying a pawl indicated at M^{15}, M^{16}, which is adapted to engage the teeth of the ratchet wheels M^{11}, M^{12}, being held in engagement therewith by springs, one of which is shown at M^{17}, secured to said pawl carrier M^{13}. Suitably mounted upon the casing M, and adapted to engage the teeth of the ratchet wheels M^{11}, M^{12}, is a detent M^{19}, to prevent reverse movement of said ratchet wheels.

The pawl carrier plate M^{13} is provided with a pin M^{21}, and secured thereby loosely to said carrier is one end of a connecting rod M^{21a}, the other end of said connecting rod being connected to one end of a longitudinally flexible coupling M^{22}, the other end of said coupling being secured by means of the connecting rod M^{23} to the power transmission lever L. The function of the flexible coupling M^{22} will be hereinafter referred to.

The pawl carrier M^{13} also carries, at its lower end, a pin N, and loosely mounted thereon is one end of a connecting rod N^1, the other end of said rod being connected to a pin N^2 secured to the pawl carrier M^{14}, whereby, when motion is imparted to pawl carrier M^{13} and, through the pawl M^{15} to the ratchet wheel M^{11}, motion is imparted to the pawl carrier M^{14}, and through its pawl M^{16} to the ratchet wheel M^{12}. From the pin N^2 is suspended a weight N^3 to return the pawl carriers to their lowermost positions when they complete their upward travel.

The flexible coupling M^{22} comprises a tubular casing N^4, which is provided at one end with an opening N^5, through which projects a rod N^6 having a head N^7, which is adapted to bear against a spiral spring N^8 mounted within said casing, the other end of said rod N^6 being connected to the rod M^{23}.

The operation of the apparatus, as thus far described, will be more readily apparent from an inspection of Fig. 5.

Assuming that the expansion coil there shown has been subject to a normal temperature of say 75 degrees Fahrenheit, and at that temperature the lever L is in the position shown in full lines on a decrease in temperature of say 10 degrees, the contraction of the coil, which will operate upon its entire length, will exert a pressure at the ends thereof in the direction of the arrows, the result of which will be to rotate the shaft J and raise the lever L against the force of the weighted lever K (carrying the latter therewith) to the position shown in dotted lines, thereby actuating the ratchet wheels M^{11}, M^{12}, and winding up the springs M^9, M^{10}, of the power-storage device, the force there stored being afterwards taken off, as required, through the medium of the power transmission shaft M^1 and spur wheel M^2 and any suitable gearing or power transmission means.

The function of the flexible coupling indicated at M^{22} will now be quite clear. It will be seen that the coil spring N^8 will be sufficiently strong not to give under the pull of the lever L except when the springs M^9, M^{10} are wound full. When that condition exists, the coil spring N^8 will give, under the force of the lever L, and

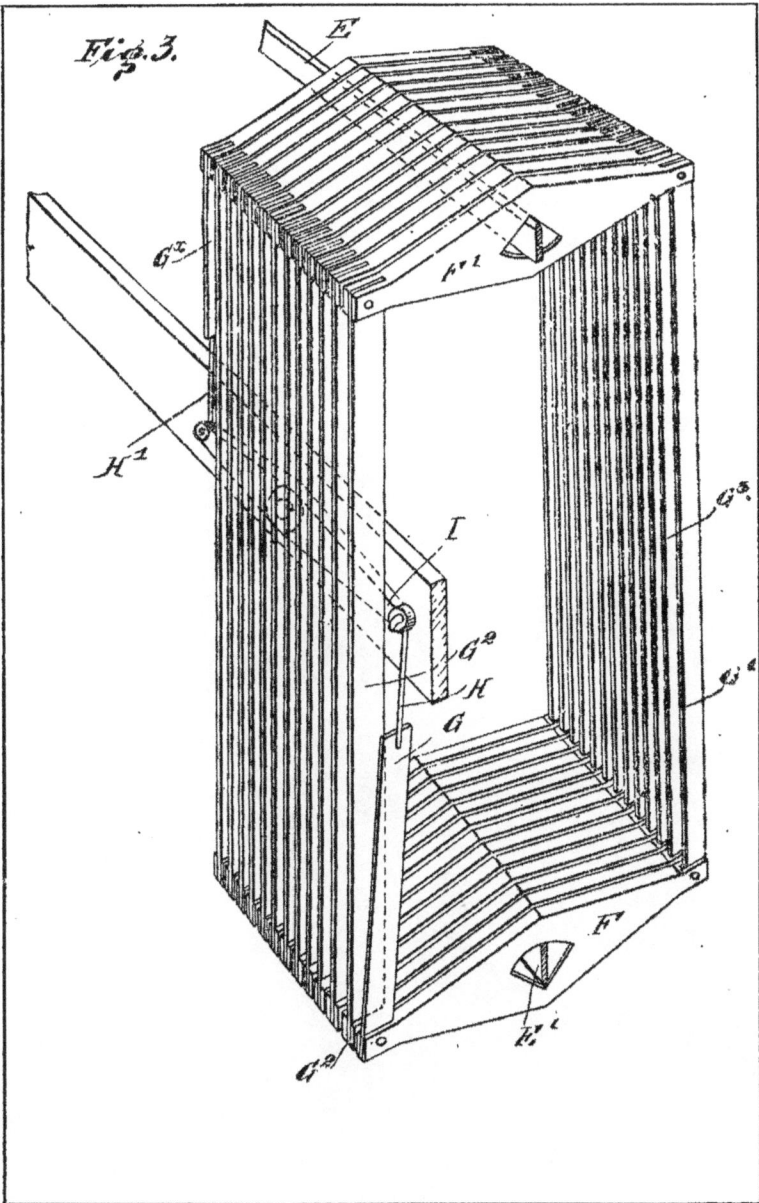

Fig. 3.

BANGERTER'S PERPETUAL TIME CLOCK

no further power will be applied to the springs M^9, M^{10}. When, however, those springs have become unwound to a sufficient extent the spring N^8 of the coupling M^{22} will be stronger than the springs of the power-storage device and will transmit, from the expansion coil, the force necessary to wind said springs as often as they become unwound; in other cases the force will be expended in simply compressing the coil spring N^8 without effect upon the springs of the power-storage device.

Referring now to what I will term the force-increasing devices, which are more clearly shown in Figs. 1, 2, 4, 8 and 9.

Near each end of the upper knife-bar E, and contacting therewith at its under surface, is a support O, in the form of a flat-headed bolt (Fig. 8), the shank of said bolt passing through one end of lever O^1, which is fulcrumed at O^2 upon the upper surface of a cross-bar O^3 securely fastened to the rear portion of the uprights C, C^1. To the front of said uprights is rigidly secured a second cross-bar O^4, and at the lower portion of said uprights and rigidly secured thereto is a third cross-bar O^5, against the under surface of which rests a lever O^6 (Fig. 9) having its fulcrum point at O^7.

As shown in Fig. 2, there are three sets of the levers O^1, at the upper end of the expansion coils at the rear side thereof below the knife-bars E, one lever at each end of said bar and one in the middle thereof. As these levers act directly upon the under surface of the knife-bars E to raise the same I will call them knife-bar lifting-levers. There are also the same number of levers O^6 at the lower end of the expansion coils below the cross-bar O^5 projecting through to the forward side of the apparatus, as shown in Fig. 1.

Rigidly secured to the cross-bar O^4 is one end of a relatively heavy metallic expansion strip O^8,—preferably formed of zinc—the lower end being secured to one end of the lever O^6; to the opposite end of the lever O^6 is secured the lower end of a similar but longer zinc strip O^9, the upper end of the strip O^9 being secured to the rear end of the lever O^1. As shown in Figs. 1 and 2, there are two of these strips O^8 at the front and two of the strips O^9 at the rear of the apparatus.

In addition to the heavy strips O^8, O^9, there is provided at the front of the apparatus a heavy wide expansion sheet or strip O^{10}, which, at its upper end, is rigidly secured to the cross-bar O^4, and at its lower end to the front end of the middle one of the levers O^6. A similar heavy wide expansion sheet or strip O^{11} is secured, at its lower end, to the rear end of the middle lever O^6, and, at its upper end, to the middle one of the levers O^1.

These heavy strips O^8, O^9 and sheets O^{10}, O^{11} are preferably formed of zinc, and are not only capable of great expansion and contraction, but will be capable by their contraction of lifting the entire weight of the knife-bars E, with the carried balance-levers and expansion strips of expansion coils, the operation thereof being as follows:

The front strips O^8 and rear strips O^9 and the front sheets O^{10} and the rear sheets O^{11} are connected to the levers O^6, so as to form, in effect, single expansion strips and sheets of relatively great length. They are fastened, however, at their front upper ends to the cross-bars O^4, so that the expansion cannot extend beyond that point and takes place in a direction towards the opposite end, and, of course, the contraction takes place in the opposite direction. Assuming now that at a temperature of say 75 degrees Fahr. these heavy strips and sheets lie in the position shown in Figs. 4 and 9 (the heavy strips O^8, O^9 being shown in Fig. 9, and the heavy wide sheets O^{10}, O^{11} in Fig. 4), on a decrease in temperature of say five degrees Fahr., the heavy strips O^8, O^9 and sheets O^{11}, O^{12} will contract in the direction of the arrows, depressing the rear ends of the levers O^1, O^6, and thereby through the levers O^1 lifting the knife-bars E, and the balance-levers suspended thereon, with the result that the force normally exerted at the ends of each expansion coil is increased to the extent of the lifting power of the contraction of the metal strips and sheets.

I have found by experiment as well as observation that the average daily change of temperature in residence and office buildings is about five degrees. Sometimes the changes will be much greater, and sometimes less. On even a low average of temperature change, my apparatus will be able to generate force in larger amounts than required, and the surplus will be stored in a power-storage device such as above described, or by means hereinafter referred to, which surplus will

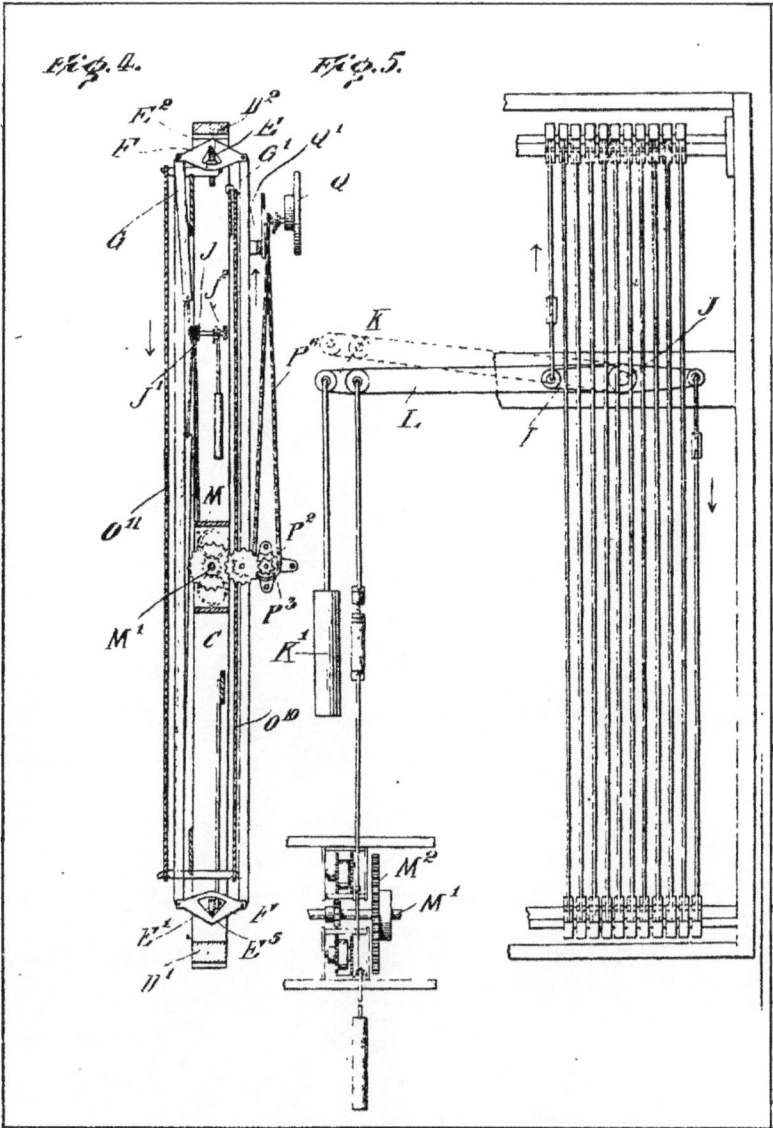

BANGERTER'S PERPETUAL TIME CLOCK

be drawn upon when it should happen that the average temperature is approximately uniform.

For clearness of illustration, I have shown, as above stated, but two sets of expansion coils, but there is no limit to the number that may be used.   Assuming that we have an apparatus with four expansion coils, each knife-bar holding 50 balance levers, giving a total of 200 levers, with expansion strips of the same number, in 5-foot lengths, we would have a total of 1,000 linear feet of zinc strips, which entire length of strips will, on the slightest change of temperature, get longer or shorter.   The expansion and contracting of this 1,000 feet of zinc strips for every temperature change of 5 degrees Fahr. will be 1 inch.   Now, assuming that the knife-bars are pulled upward by heavy strips O^8, O^9, and sheets O^{10}, O^{11} of five feet length (making ten feet for the front and rear strips and sheets), on a decrease in temperature of 5 degrees Fahr. the upward movement of those bars will be 10-1000 of one inch; this contraction (10-1000) will now be multiplied as many times as there are levers and strips in the expansion coils, viz., 200 times, which would be 2 inches, and this, together with 1 inch from the contraction of the expansion coils alone, will give a total movement of 3 inches.   If the strips are of a capacity to pull or lift 100 pounds, we obtain a lift of 100 pounds 3 inches.   As thirty-three per cent approximately must be deducted for loss by stress (it being necessary to place the coils under strain, as shown in the drawings and described above), the final result will be a power to lift 100 pounds 2 inches, or 10 pounds 20 inches, and this force will be sufficient to run a large sized time clock with powerful striking force.

As illustrated in Figs. 4, 5, 6 and 7, the power applied by the springs M^9, M^{10} to the power transmission shaft M^1 is taken, through the spur wheel M^2 by means of any suitable gearing, to run a clock or any other machine adapted to the purpose.   As there illustrated, I show the spur wheel M^2 meshing with a pinion P, through which is driven the spur wheel P^1, which latter meshes with a pinion P^2, through which is driven a sprocket wheel P^3 carried by the bracket P^4, which latter, as well as the shafts carrying said spur wheels and pinions, are supported by an upright P^5 mounted upon the casing M. The sprocket wheel P^3 carries a sprocket chain P^6, which, through any suitable gearing, is adapted to wind the main spring of a clock indicated at Q, carried by suitable supports on the cross-bar Q¹ secured to the uprights C, C¹. As this clock may be of any well known form, it will not be necessary to describe the same in detail, except to state that as soon as the main spring of the clock becomes weaker than the springs of the power-storage device illustrated in Fig. 7, the latter will wind the clock main spring, and as in this manner it is wound frequently, it is always kept at a uniform high tension, which is desirable and results in good timekeeping.

In Fig. 12 I show a modification of my invention, wherein, instead of having the balance-levers F, F¹ arranged side by side, they are superposed one above the other, in this case a plurality of knife-bars E, E¹ also being superposed one above the other, the expansion strips G, G¹, etc. (in this case shown as formed of wires or rods), and balance-levers being arranged in the same plane, somewhat in the nature of a coiled spring, the coil shaft being indicated at J and the coil lever at I, to which are connected the end expansion strips G, Gˣ, and the weight K¹ for placing the coil under tension. By this arrangement of balance-levers and expansion strips, in the same plane, much economy of space is effected, and when desired, a great number of such coils may be suspended upon the series of knife-bars.

In Fig. 12ᵃ I show two such coils connected in series, the terminal expansion strip Gˣ of the front coil being connected to one end of the lever I, and the opposite terminal G of that coil being connected to the shortest one of the rear set of levers F¹ᵃ, the terminal Gʸ of the rear set being connected to the other end of the lever I. Thus two or more such coils may be connected, and the force of expansion and contraction of the combined coils transmitted to the lever I. When a number of such combined coils are suspended from the knife-bars E, E¹, the levers connecting their respective terminals may be themselves connected by a system of compound levers such, for example, as shown in Fig. 13, to be hereinafter referred to.

Referring now to Figs. 13 to 20 inclusive. These figures illustrate another form of the invention whereby not only the power-storage device of the preceding fig-

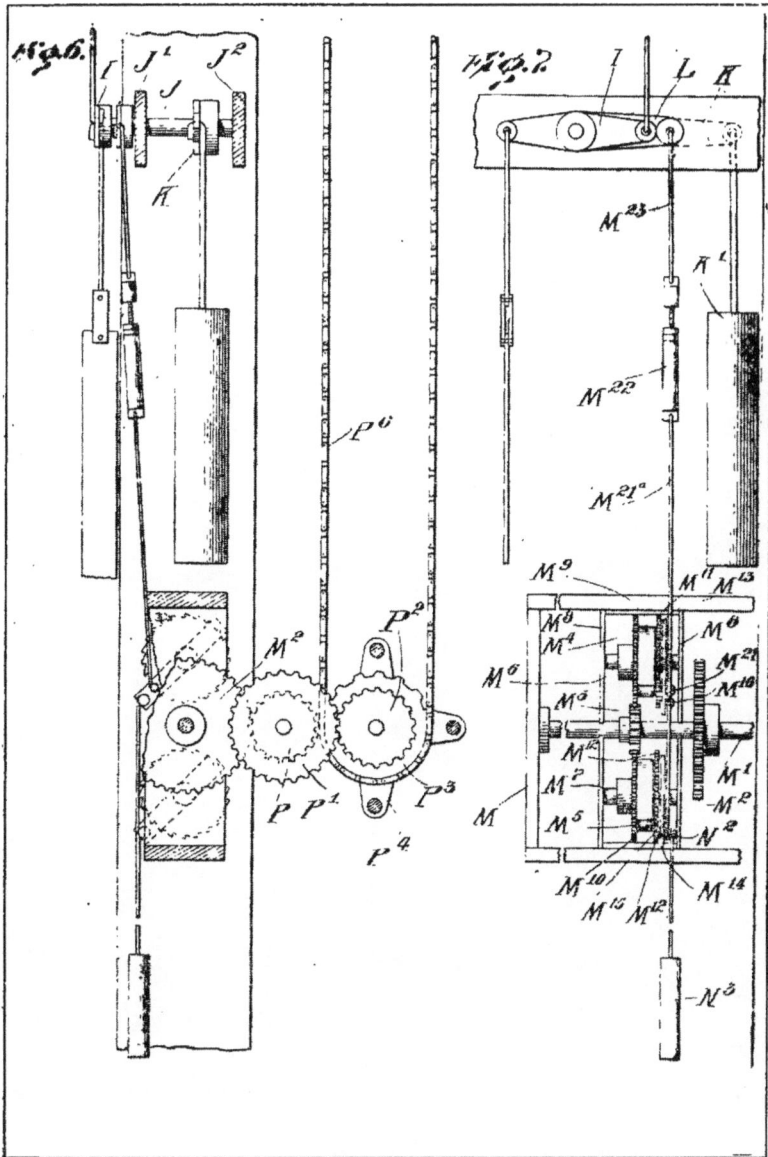

BANGERTER'S PERPETUAL TIME CLOCK

ures may be dispensed with, but also the main spring of the clock there shown, both of these elements being supplanted by apparatus effecting the raising and lowering of weights (in this instance shown in the form of balls), the force of expansion and contraction of the coils being utilized to operate a rotary member which elevates a series of weights and discharges the same into a storage receiver, the clock (or other machine) being operated through the energy so stored and given up by the falling of said weights.

As illustrated in said figures, this feature of the invention consists of a frame, indicated in whole at 10, located about midway the length of the expansion coils shown in Fig. 1, and it may be supported by securing it to the uprights C, C^1, or in any other suitable manner.

Said frame comprises two horizontally disposed longitudinal framing members, 10^a, 10^b, which are connected at each end by cross-bars (not shown).

Mounted on the supports 10^a, 10^b, are four uprights, 12^a, 12^b, 13^a, 13^b. The uprights 12^a 12^b are connected at their upper ends by a longitudinal framing member 14^a, and the uprights 13^a 13^b are connected by longitudinal framing member 14^b, said framing members 14^a 14^b being also in turn connected at their ends by transverse bars (not shown), said members constituting an open frame for the working parts of the apparatus.

Mounted respectively upon the longitudinal framing members 10^a 10^b, approximately midway thereof, are two standards, 16^a 16^b, which are rigidly secured together by a cross-bar 17, said standards and cross-bar constituting a rigid support for the gearing now to be described.

Rotatably mounted upon the standards 16^a, 16^b is a driving shaft 18, one end of which is journaled in the standard 16^a, and the other end in a bearing-bolt 19 passing through the standard 16^b, which, being threaded, is capable of fine adjustment.

Mounted upon and keyed to the shaft 18 is a wheel 19, the spokes 20 of which support a rim 21, within which are set a series of pockets 22, the inner surfaces of which are so shaped as to permit their receiving successively, at the bottom of the wheel, a series of balls 23 and holding the same during a travel of 180 degrees, or one-half revolution of the wheel, when they are discharged as hereinafter described.   This wheel I will term an energy-storing wheel, since it acts through the force taken from the expansion coils to raise the balls, the lowering of which is to drive the wheel now to be described.

Loosely mounted on the shaft 18 is a wheel 24, smaller in diameter than the wheel 19, the spokes 25 of which, secured to the hub 26, support a rim 27, within which are set a series of pockets 28, which are adapted to receive successively, at the top of the wheel, the balls 23, and discharge the same when they have been lowered through 180 degrees or, in other words, at the bottom of the wheel. The inner wall of the pockets 28 is formed, for the most part, with a pronounced rounded groove (indicated at 28^a), as shown above the ball in Fig. 18, which groove lies under the ball when the pocket is in its uppermost position, as shown in Fig. 17, said groove becoming less pronounced at one edge towards the opposite portion of the pocket, at which point it has an approximately level surface at one side, as shown in Fig. 18, and indicated at 28^b; the subject of this arrangement being that the ball may be readily discharged in this position, and securely held within the pocket when the ball and pocket are in other positions.   The wheel 24—which I will designate as the power-transmission wheel—is supported upon ball bearings indicated at 28^c, 28^d, which are held in position by collars 28^e, 28^f, both keyed to shaft 18.

Mounted upon a collar 29, which is keyed to the driving shaft 18, is a ratchet wheel 30, engaging the teeth of which are two pawls 31, 32, secured to one arm of a double-arm pawl-carrier 33, the other arm of which is connected by a rod 34 to a lever 35, one end of which lever is pivotally connected to a standard 36, secured to the frame, and the other end of which is provided with a weight 36^a.

Near the inner end of the lever 35 connection is made by means of the connecting rods 37 and 38, link 39 and rods 40, 41, with two levers indicated at L, L, which are adapted to take power from the expansion coils heretofore described, through the coil shafts J, J, to which shafts are also connected the coil levers I, I, the ends of the latter being connected to the strips G, G^x of the expansion coil by the wires H, H^1, as already set forth and clearly illustrated in Figs. 2, 3, 5, 6 and 7.

As illustrated in Fig. 13, upon contraction of the ex-

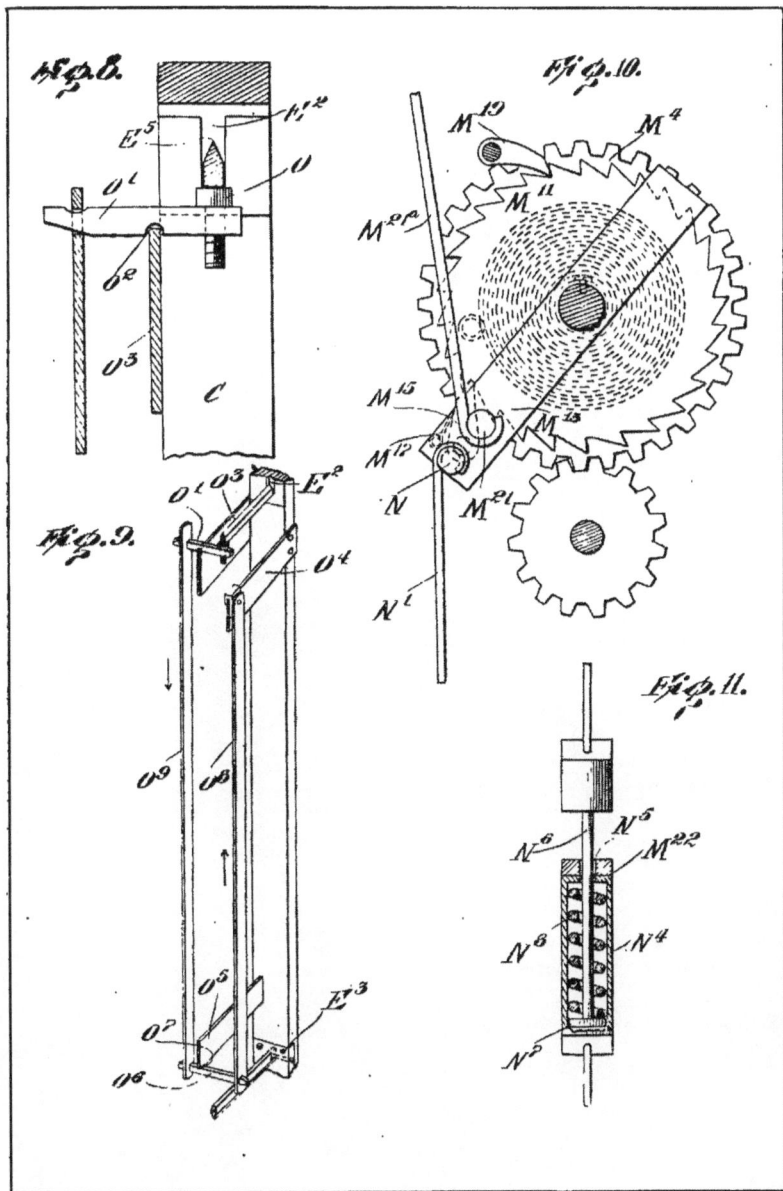

BANGERTER'S PERPETUAL TIME CLOCK

pansion coils, the wires H, H¹ will be pulled in the direction indicated by the arrows, the ends of the long arms of the levers L, L—through the movement of the shafts J, J—will rise, thereby, through the rods 40, 41, link 39 and rods 38, 37, raising the lever 35, and through the rod 34 actuating the pawl carrier 33, and through the pawls 31, 32, imparting rotary motion to the ratchet wheel 30, and, through it, to the shaft 18 and the power-storing wheel 19, said pawl carrier being returned to its normal position by the weight 36ª. Motion of said wheel and shaft in the reverse direction is prevented by means of a ratchet wheel 42, keyed to the collar 29, engaging the teeth of which wheel is a detent 43, carried by a plate 44, secured to the supports 45, affixed to the standard 16ª.

The hub member 26 of the power transmission wheel 24 is provided with a sprocket wheel 46, which is adapted to engage and drive a sprocket chain 47, and thereby drive the great wheel of a clock mechanism or gearing of any other machine adapted to the purpose.

Having shown the mechanism for driving the energy-storing wheel 19, which, as already stated, is keyed to the shaft 18, I will now describe the mechanism for driving the power transmission wheel 24, which runs loose on the shaft 18.

It will be seen from an inspection of Fig. 16 that the wheel 19 is of greater diameter than the wheel 24.

Suitably mounted between said wheels, on cross-bars 48, 49, I provide a series of ball-storage runways designated in whole at 50 (see Fig. 14), and, as shown in Fig. 16, these runways are laterally inclined downwardly from the wheel 19 to the wheel 24.

Similar ball runways designated in whole at 51 are provided at the lower portion of said wheels and between the same (Fig. 20), being mounted upon cross-bars 52, 53, but the last named runways are laterally inclined in the reverse direction to that of the runways 50.

The ball-storage runways 50 comprise inclined floor members 54, 54ª, 54ᵇ, each having longitudinally a slight downward inclination in the direction of the arrows. These runways also comprise longitudinally extending walls 55, 56, 57, 58, one end of the wall 55 being curved to meet one end of the wall 57, leaving a passageway 59 between it and one end of the wall 56. One end of the wall 58 is similarly curved to meet one end of the wall 56, leaving a passageway 60 between it and one end of the wall 57. Thus are provided parallel runways 61, 62 and 63, with passageways from one to the other, whereby a ball deposited in runway 61 will move continuously from that end of the series of runways to the other end. The runway 61 is provided with an end wall 61^a, and adjacent thereto the longitudinal wall 55 is provided with an opening 61^b to permit the passage therethrough successively of balls from the energy-storing wheel 19 to the runway 61.

Projecting through the standard 16^b is a threaded bolt 63^a, the end of the shank of which is beveled, as clearly shown in Figs. 14 and 16, the function of which is to eject from the uppermost pocket 22 of the wheel 19, as the same revolves, the balls 23, and thrust them successively into the runway 61.

At the lower end of the runway 63 is provided a laterally movable receptacle 64, which has a receiving capacity of one ball only. Said receptacle comprises a base 65 and perpendicular stop 66. The base 65 is connected to the floor member 54^b of the runway 63 by a horizontally disposed hinge 67, and to it is also affixed a plate 68, carrying a downwardly extending lever arm 69, which is formed at its lower extremity with an outwardly curving portion 70, which is adapted to engage with the spokes 25 of the wheel 24 and be thereby pressed inwardly, the result of which is to depress the outer end of the base 65 of the ball receptacle 64, inclining the same in such position that the ball therein will fall into the adjacent pocket of the wheel 24, the ball being prevented from falling therefrom on the opposite side by the stop 71 secured to the standard 16^a. The center of gravity of the lever arm 69 is such that when the curved lower portion is in its normal forwardly extended position the rear side of the base 65 of the receptacle 64 will be depressed and the forward side elevated, so that the forward side will normally project above the floor level of the runway 63 and serve as a stop to prevent more than one ball occupying any of the space within said receptacle at one time.

The ball-storage runways 51 comprise inclined floor members 72, 72^a, 72^b, each having a slight downward inclination longitudinally in the direction of the arrows. They also comprise longitudinally extending walls 73,

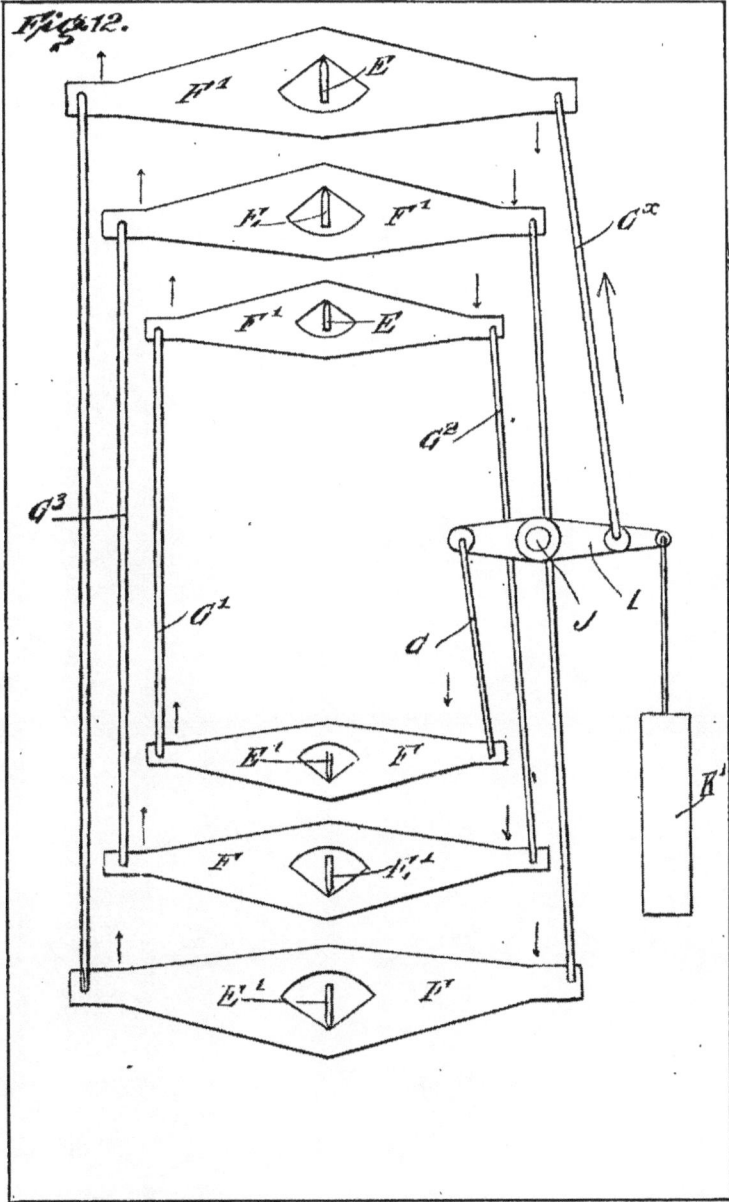

Fig. 12.

BANGERTER'S PERPETUAL TIME CLOCK

74, 75 and 76, one end of the wall 73 being curved to meet one end of the wall 75, leaving a passageway 77 between it and one end of the wall 74. One end of the wall 76 is similarly curved to meet one end of the wall 74, leaving a passageway 78 between it and the other end of the wall 75. There are thus formed parallel runways 79, 80 and 81, with passageways from one to the other, whereby a ball deposited at the other end of the runway 79 will move continuously from that end of the series of runways to the other end. The runway 79 is provided with an end wall 82, and adjacent thereto the longitudinal wall 76 is provided with an opening 76^a to permit the passage therethrough, at intervals, of balls from the power-transmission wheel 24 to the runway 79. Adjacent the wall 82 is perpendicularly disposed pin 82^a whereby the balls, as they pass through the opening in the wall 76 are deflected to pass through the runway 79 in the direction of the arrow.

At the lower end of the runway 81 is provided a laterally movable receptacle 83, which has a receiving capacity for one ball only. Said receptacle comprises a base 84 and end stop 85. Said receptacle is horizontally hinged at 86 to the floor member 72 of the runway 81, and is provided with an outward extension 87, which is adapted to be engaged by a shoulder 88 on the ball pockets 22, and thereby depress the outer edge of the base of the receptacle in such a way as to eject the ball therefrom, and place the same in the pocket of the wheel 19.

It will be seen that the hinge 86 (Fig. 19) is off center and when the base 84 of the receptacle 83 is depressed at the rear the upper end of a pin 89, projecting upwardly from the base 84 contacts with the upper portion of the wall 74, thereby preventing the rear portion of the base being depressed too low. When a ball is in said receptacle, the forward end will be elevated so that a portion of the side edge of the base will be projected above the floor member of the runway 81, serving as a stop to prevent more than one ball occupying any of the space within said receptacle. When one ball moves into a pocket 22, another ball quickly moves into the receptacle, taking its position at the rear thereof. This operation takes place when the base 84 is level with the floor member of the runway 81, the outer end of the base rising as soon as the pocket and its ball have passed by the projection 87.

It will be seen that the energy-storing wheel 19, which takes its motive power through the shaft 18 from the expansion coils, acts to raise the balls or weights from the lower ball runways 51 to the ball storage runways 50. The wheel 19 may act at more or less irregular intervals, while the power transmission wheel 24 acts—and must act—continuously and regularly. This wheel takes and transmits power from the lowering of the balls, which are delivered to it when the pockets are in the position of the one shown uppermost in Fig. 15, and are discharged from the pockets when in the position of the one shown lowermost in said figure, in which position of the wheel the approximately flat surface of the pocket (Fig. 18) is lowermost, or under the ball, permitting ready discharge of same. From the delivery side of the power transmission wheel 24 the balls are discharged into the runway 79, being deflected into proper direction by the pin 83ª, thence passing through the passageway 78 through the runway 80 in the direction of the arrow, thence through the opening 77 into the runway 81, thence into receptacle 83, and when the shoulder 88 of the energy-storing wheel 19 reaches a point opposite said receptacle the base of the latter is depressed, which results in passing a ball into the wheel pocket; as the wheel turns and the next pocket arrives in position another ball is taken on, and so on, as long as there are any balls in the lower runway. When a ball on the wheel 19 reaches the uppermost position, as shown in Fig. 16, it contacts with the ejector 63ª and is thereby passed into the runway 61 and thence to the lower end of that series of runways, and in the same way the balls following will take position in the upper series of runways.

It will be understood that when my invention is applied to the operation of a clock the power taken from the power transmission wheel 24 will be given up gradually, being controlled by the pendulum or balance wheel governed escapement in the usual way.

In the application of my invention as last above described the apparatus will be designed and built to furnish energy sufficient not only to run the clock, but provide a surplus for storage. On some days the variation in temperature may be but two or three degrees, and on

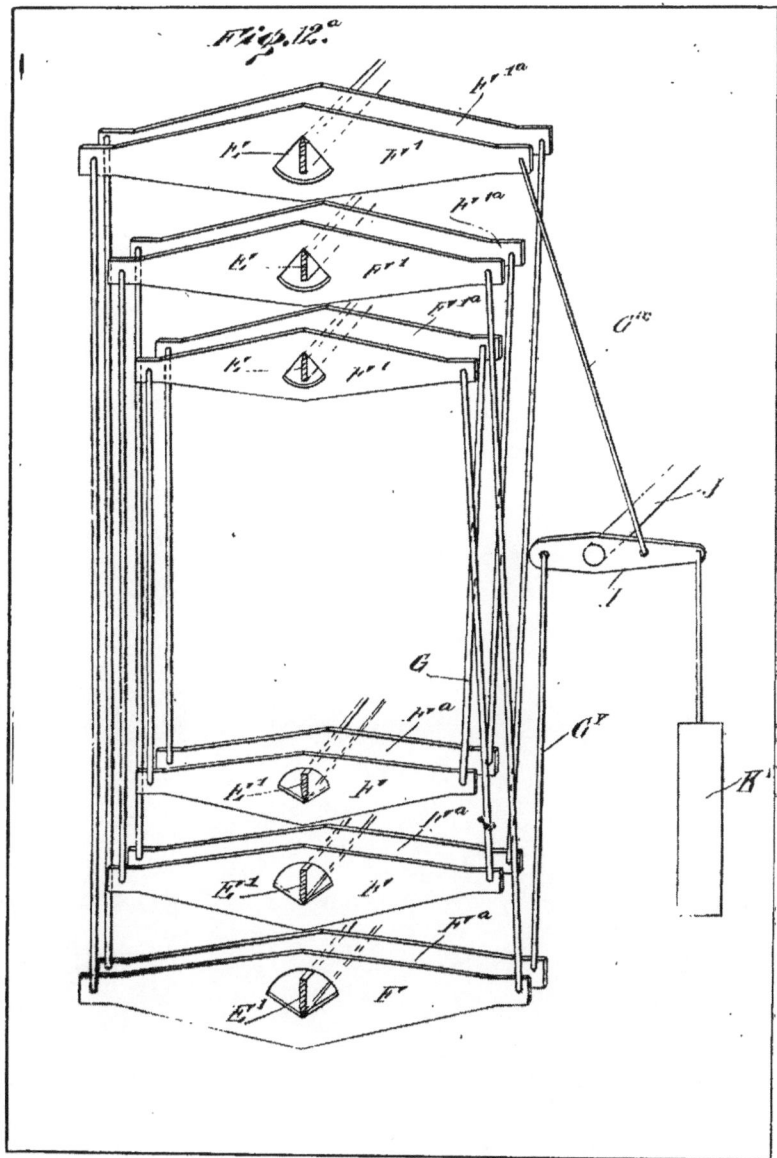

BANGERTER'S PERPETUAL TIME CLOCK

other days it may be as high as twenty degrees.   If the clock requires for its operation the lowering of three balls each day the apparatus will be so arranged that with an average daily temperature variation of, say, six degrees, four balls will be raised, of which three will operate the power transmission wheel and one will be held in storage. With a variation of twelve degrees, eight balls will be raised, of which five balls will be left in storage.   If the ball storage runways each have a holding capacity for one hundred balls, and the variation in temperature is greater than required, the balls will soon be lifted from the lower to the upper runways.   Assuming that on certain days there will be no variation in temperature, and as a result the energy-storing wheel should not revolve, the running of the clock will not be interrupted, for the power transmission wheel will continue revolving, taking its power from the balls in storage.

I wish it understood that I do not confine myself to the precise details of construction and arrangement of parts as herein set forth and described or to the materials specified, as modification and variation may be made without departing from the spirit of the invention as defined by the appended claims.

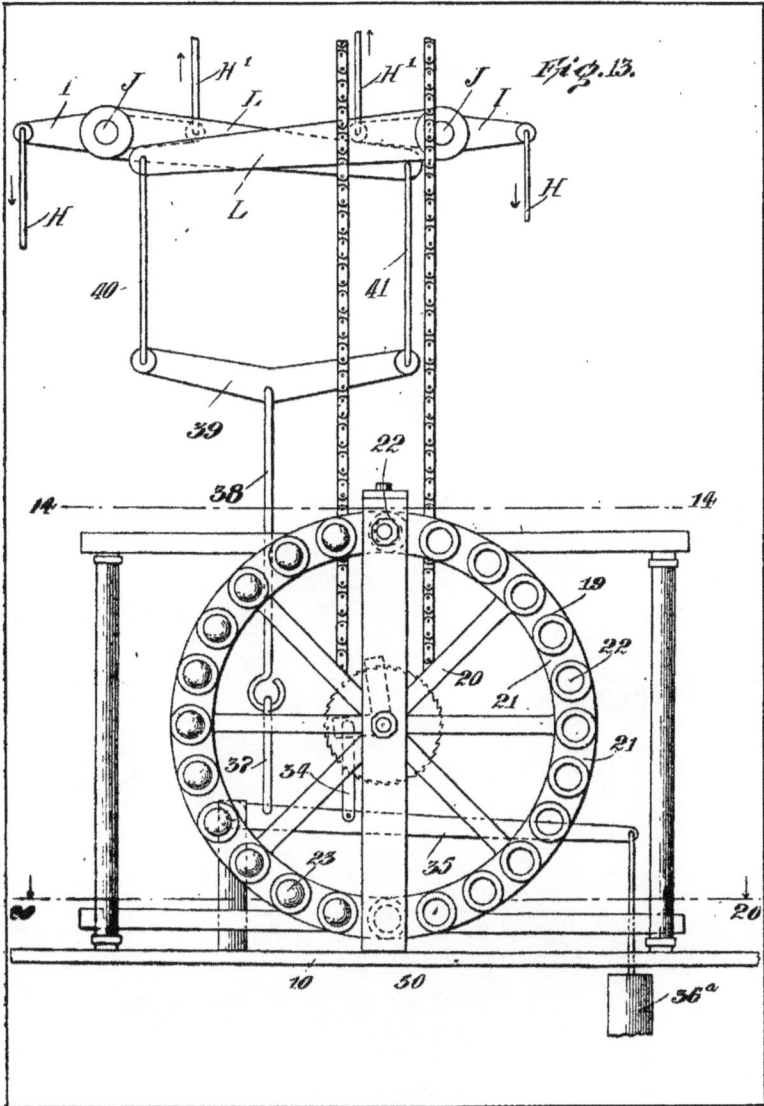

Fig. 13.

BANGERTER'S PERPETUAL TIME CLOCK

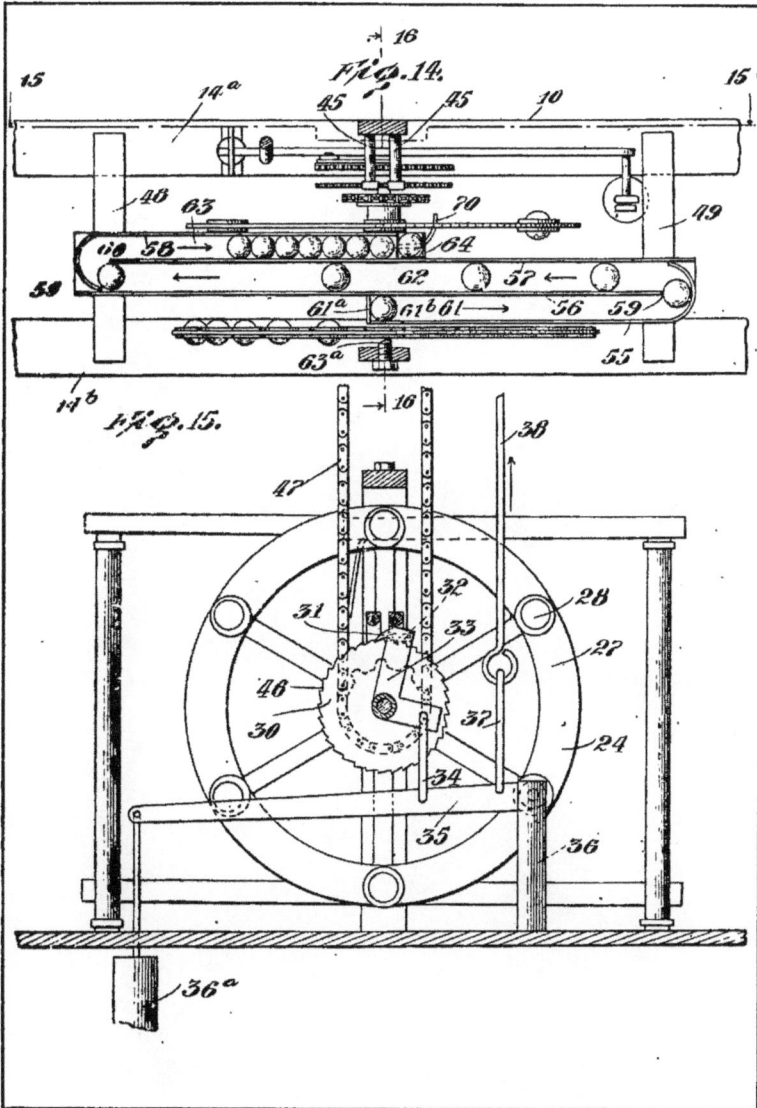

BANGERTER'S PERPETUAL TIME CLOCK

BANGERTER'S PERPETUAL TIME CLOCK

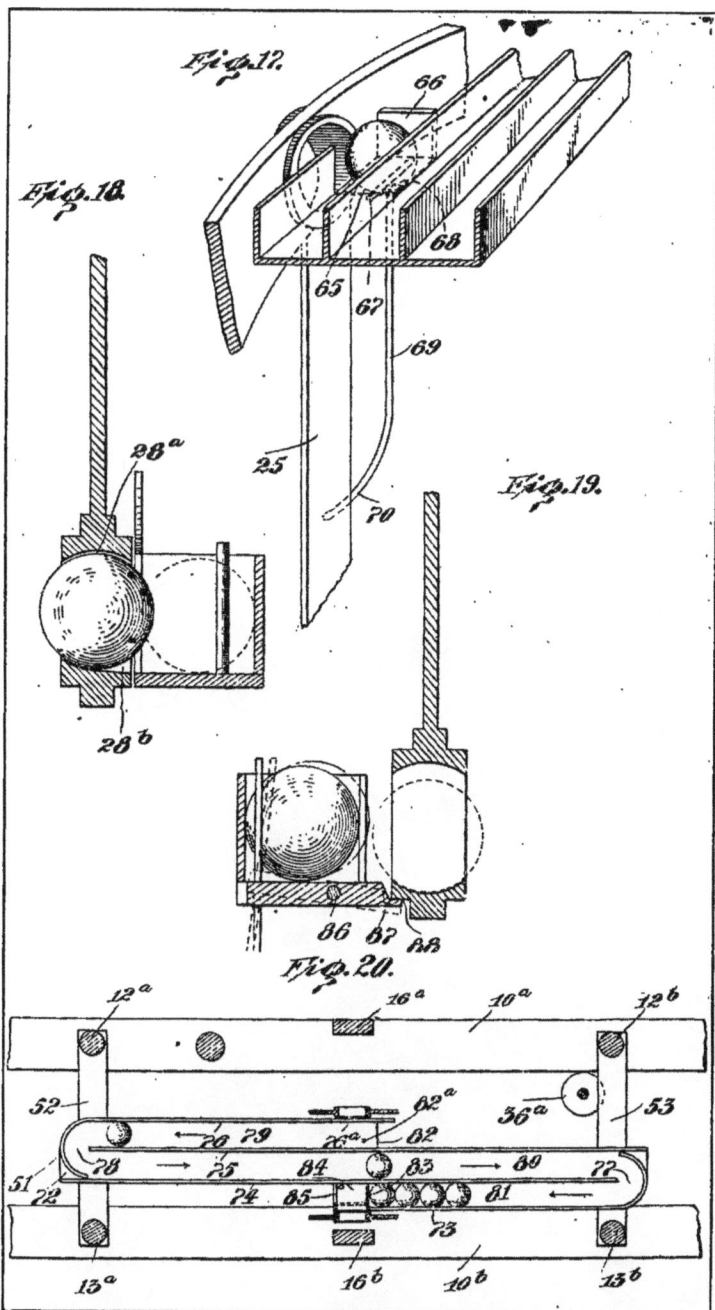

BANGERTER'S PERPETUAL TIME CLOCK

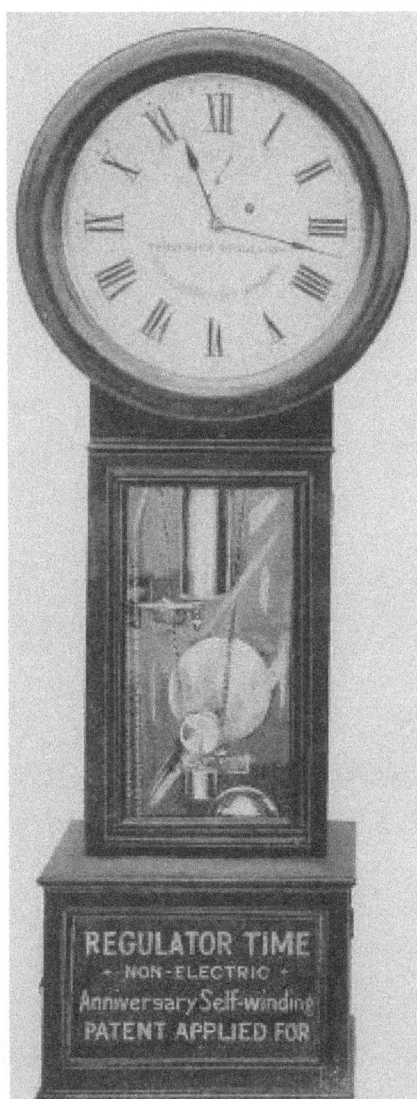

BANGERTER'S NON-ELECTRIC REGULATOR TIME
CLOCK—ANNIVERSARY SELF-WINDING.

Patent Applied for, 1911.

BANGERTER'S NON-ELECTRIC REGULATOR TIME CLOCK
ANNIVERSARY SELF-WINDING

The Bangerter Anniversary Self-Winding Regulator deserves this title because its construction embodies all the principles essential to a Regulator to be the very best time-keeper. "Graham dead-beat escapement" and a pendulum provided with means for keeping its gravity always the same length, overcoming the variation which change in temperature invariably brings about.

Another great improvement is the daily Self-Winding System, winding a weight which is the only means of maintaining an even pull to the delicate works of the clock. Wound by a force which requires attention one minute a year only.

This invention relates to clocks, and particularly that class wherein a pendulum escapement is employed and wherein the clock-train is weight driven.

It is well known to those skilled in the art that the most accurate and reliable clocks are those which are driven by a weight. Most of such clocks are provided with a plurality of weights, one being used to supply the energy necessary to strike the time, and the other the energy for operating the clock-train, and in clocks of such construction they have to be wound frequently, usually either daily or weekly.

Many attempts have been made to produce clocks which will run for a relatively long time without requiring the attention of an attendant to wind the same. In such clocks (other than electrical clocks) powerful springs have been employed, one of such springs being used for time-striking and the other for actuating the clock-train. Clocks of this class designed to run for an extended length of time, such, for example, as period of, say, a year or more, have been indifferent time-keepers, due to the fact that the power of the springs becomes materially lessened during the latter part of the cycle of operations. Therefore, spring-operated clocks, calculated to be run for any great length of time, have been more or less unsatisfactory, and have not gone into very extensive use.

The object of my invention is to provide a clock which will not require the attention of an attendant but once in a long period of time, and which will also be an accurate time-keeper.

A further object is to provide a clock operated by a uniformly pulling weight, the pull of which is not varied by the lifting of said weight.

A further object is to provide a power-storage device and power transmission mechanism and automatic devices connected thereto, whereby the power of said power-storage mechanism is utilized to wind up the clock—that is to say, to lift the clock-train operating weight at certain definitely recurring intervals of time.

A further object of my invention is to provide, in connection with such power-storage mechanism, time-striking means operated by said power-storage device, which being independent of the clock-train operating means does not interfere therewith.

A further object of my invention is to provide a single power-storage mechanism which will afford the power to strike the time and effect the winding of the clock, doing away with two sets of mechanism (one for each purpose), as heretofore used.

A further object of my invention is to provide such a power-storage device that with one winding of the same the clock may be kept running, and also striking the time, for a year or more in duration.

A further object of my invention is to provide means in connection with said power-storage device whereby 'the winding of the clock-train does not interfere with continuous running and perfect time-keeping of the clock, and does not require any supplemental propelling mechanism for the clock-train during the winding operation.

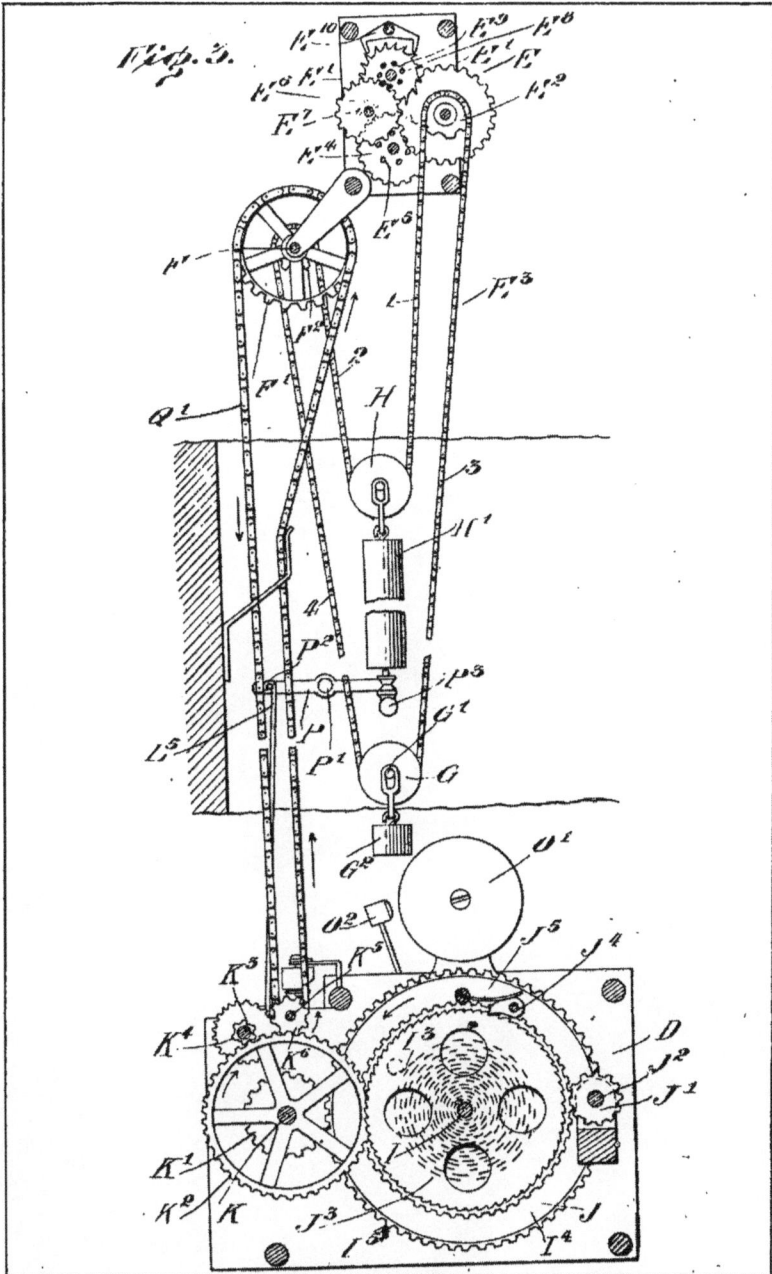

DRAWING OF BANGERTER'S SELF-WINDING CLOCK.

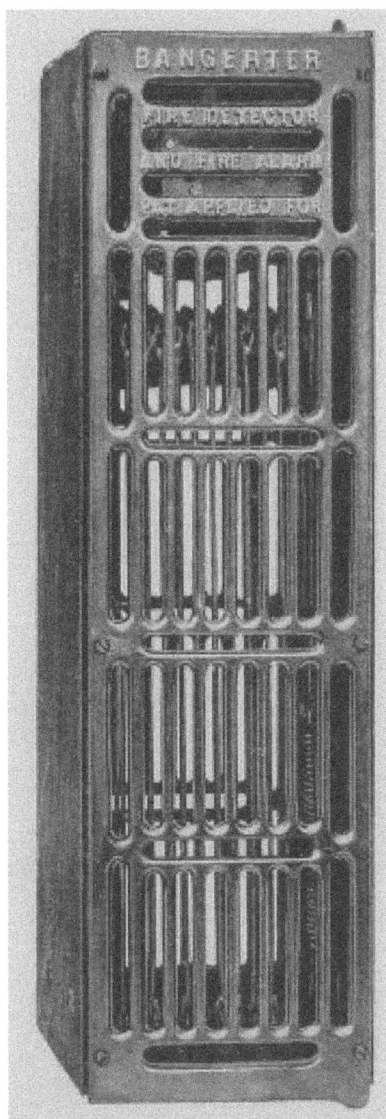

BANGERTER'S FIRE DETECTOR AND FIRE ALARM.

This is the most marvelous little machine that science has ever devised to watch your house day and night. It is the truest of all Watch Dogs and will in case of fire make such a loud and noisy alarm that you will wake up from the deepest of sleeps. It calls when the fire is at its infancy, in time to save you and your beloved ones. It is a most simple little apparatus requiring no electricity, no wiring or connections, no care of any kind; just as reliable after it has been hanging in your room for twenty years as it was when newly installed.

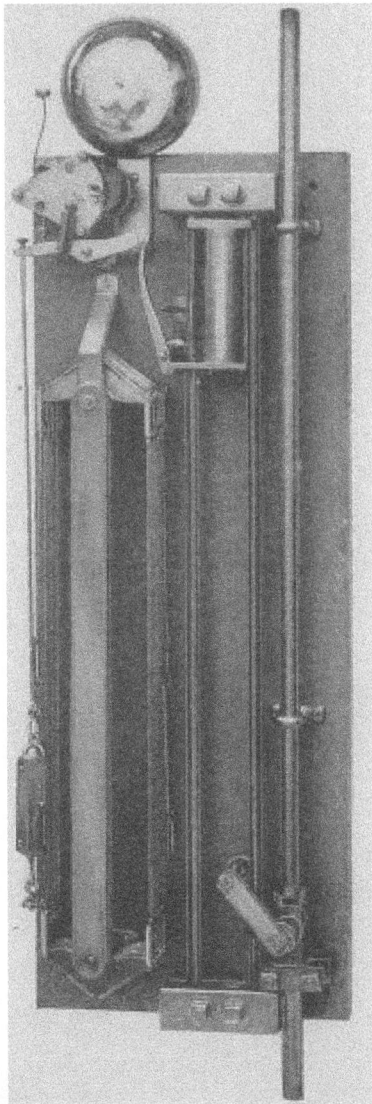

BANGERTER'S FIRE ALARM AND SPRINKLER.

More than a hundred million dollars is the yearly loss by fire in the United States; 50 per cent. of this loss is by water. How important therefore is Bangerter's "Watch Dog Fire Alarm and Sprinkler," regulated to ring, first a loud call when a fire is in its infancy. A watchman or anyone hearing the call can rush to the place and extinguish the fire. The sprinkler will only work when the alarm call is not attended to. Our Fire Alarm and Sprinkler system can be connected to piping from the water main, or to the tank on the roof of a building, but can also be installed in any place if there should be no water piping or tank. In this case a water tank of from twenty to one hundred gallons of water has to be installed. This tank can be set in any out of the way place. Compressed air keeps this water under high pressure, and in case of fire the valves are automatically opened and the sprinkler will act with efficacious result.

BRIEF BIOGRAPHY

OF

FRIEDRICH BANGERTER

Friedrich Bangerter can justly lay claim to being one of this country's leading inventors.

He has some fifty inventions to his credit.

He has been honored with Silver and Gold Medals and Diplomas.

His displays at great World's Expositions have occasioned the utmost favorable comment.

His splendid record speaks for itself and shows the profound student, the practical machinist and brainy inventor of worldwide experience with a long list of successes to his credit.

Born in Lyss, Switzerland, in 1868, at the age of 16 he entered the machine shop of his town's watch factory as an apprentice. There he was favored with the opportunity to become familiar with all sorts of tools and machines used in making watches.

By the age of 22 he so progressed that "all by himself" he constructed all the necessary machines to make watches and added so many important improvements, embracing such automatic devices and machines in which hands, moving from place to place, picking up pieces of work, then setting them in the right positions (operating with such perfection and precision) that he was called a wizard. One of these automatic machines would pick up blanks from a wire, set them in the machine from one to twenty-four at a time and cut the teeth of watch gearing perfectly.

Another of Bangerter's machines would take small, smooth, round steel rods and automatically make perfectly finished pinions with pivots, shoulders and smallest holes.

An automatic trumpet of his invention would play a complete tune and was so simple in operation that a one-year-old child, by simply blowing in it, could play it.

United States Patent 543668 for a Hair Clipper. issued to F. Bangerter, San Francisco, is specified as follows:—

543668. Hair Clipper. Fred Bangerter, San Francisco, Cal., assignor, by mesne assignments, to Charles H. Greene, same place. Filed July 21, 1894. Renewed July 2, 1895. Serial No. 554,715. (No model.)

Claim 1. In a Hair Clipper, the combination of the stationary and movable plates, a pair of pivoted handles, one of said handles being hinged or connected with one of said plates so that the device may be turned to different angles, an opposing plate having its rear portion recessed and provided with rearwardly and upwardly extending curved arms, and the other handle having arms adapted to enter the recess of said plate and engage the curved arms thereof in whatever position the device is turned.

In 1892 he exhibited an automatic figure in a big department store in San Francisco which drew a complete portrait of Christopher Columbus.

United States Patent 512089 was issued to Mr. Bangerter for an "Automatic Delineating Machine," a toy doll which would correctly write the complete alphabet. Later he so improved this figure that it could spell and talk while writing.

At the Paris Exposition in 1900 he exhibited a most remarkable machine which made collar buttons. Three rods of metal were used at the same time—one to make the head of the button, one the bottom or base, and the other the stud. The three parts of the collar button were perfectly made and finished.

The head was drilled and tapped, the stud was threaded and screwed into the head while spun into the base or bottom. The manufactured collar buttons fell into a box at the rate of 300 an hour—thus effecting a great economy of metal.

In 1905, at the Belgium Exposition, he displayed an intensely interesting novelty—an "Automatic Jeweler" —which, with arm and hand, operated an ordinary machine which turned out perfectly made collar buttons of which thousands were sold within the Exposition Grounds.

A most marvelous contrivance was his four-spindle

BANGERTER'S AUTOMATIC FOUR SPINDLE WATCH
CHAIN MACHINE,
Composed of Over Three Thousand Parts.

automatic watch chain machine composed of over three thousand parts.

This machine made from wire of four different metals, namely, gold, silver, nickel and German silver, being fed into the machine at the same time would automatically make four watch chains of four different patterns completely and properly finished. The chain itself, an invention of Mr. Bangerter, was called the Bangerter Chain. Patent sold in France.

BANGERTER'S POWDERLESS GUN.

Invention which THE LONDON DAILY TELE-GRAPH calls the Bangerter Gun, a marvel and masterpiece for war.

NEW YORK HERALD:—

Automatic Invention Operated by Secret Mechanical Power Is Tested at Stapleton, S. I.

A working model of an automatic machine gun which, it is said, will discharge bullets over a range of a mile or more at the rate of one million an hour, with a muzzle velocity of more than 3,000 feet per second, and operated by a secret mechanical power, was demonstrated yesterday by the inventor, Friedrich Bangerter.

The model, which was built to shoot a three-eighth-inch bullet, was mounted behind a partition in the factory at 79 Broad St., Stapleton, S. I. All the motive parts were covered by a tarpaulin, and the machine was run by an electric motor, connected with the gun by a belt.

The muzzle was pointed through a hole in a partition, and the observers having gathered behind a screen, the motor was started.

The target, a pine board, was placed sixty feet away. As the motor began to hum the operator turned a little wheel and a steady stream of bullets poured from the muzzle of the gun like a stream of water from the nozzle of a hose. The target seemed to melt before the eyes as all the missiles struck it, and in about 10 seconds the entire centre of the board had disappeared. This model was built for round bullets, but the inventor says that on a standard make gun, which will have a half-inch bore, conical bullets will be fired and the barrels, of which there will be two, will be rifled.

The principal use of the new gun, according to the inventor's claim, will be for operating against airships, and, as there is no recoil, he says, the gun can be pointed toward any point of the compass.

NEW YORK TIMES:—

A Wonderful Gun.—A million bullets an hour can be fired without powder. . . . It really does shoot. . . . Reporters see wooden targets torn to bits, but the inventor won't let them see the works.

A gun that can shoot one million bullets per hour at a cost of $20, that uses neither powder nor compressed air, and that fires bullets that do not require shells, was shot for the enlightenment of a delegation of New York reporters yesterday afternoon. The reporters saw the gun shoot, but they were not permitted to see that part of the gun out of which the little steel bullets came with such rapidity. The exhibition was in the factory building at No. 79 Broad street, Stapleton, S. I. In a little room adjoining that in which were placed the reporters was the gun. There were targets made of a series of big boards arranged about a foot behind one in front of it. There were four targets.

At 4 p. m. the shooting began. The first of the targets was dragged into position. A moment later the motor started up, then the bullets started to fly. They riddled the target into a pile of splinters a foot high, and they did it in less than a minute. All in all, it was estimated that 15,000 bullets pierced the targets. Not only the first of the targets was riddled into a shapeless mass, but each of the other three as well.

The reporters were permitted then to enter the gun-room. They saw a motor, from the wheel of which a belt was operated. The belt connected the motor with another wheel, which was a part of the mechanism of the gun, on top of which was a covering out of which the bullets came. They also saw the hoppers on either side of the gun into which the bullets are poured as they are needed. The reporters asked to see the gun in operation. The inventor ordered another target swung into position. There was another whirl and a second storm of bullets struck the target. The fusillade lasted about ten seconds. Again was the target demolished. The

BANGERTER'S DOLL WRITING, DESIGNING, TALKING
AND SINGING.

A Great Combination of Cams and Levers.

inventor refused to say anything about what was under the covering in the little gun-room.

Wall Street brokers had offered Mr. Bangerter the necessary capital to build a standard size gun, but Mr. Bangerter soon found out that their plans were to get the secret of his invention and take it from him.   He therefore separated from these brokers and has had nothing to do with them since.   He has kept his secrets and has remained true to the words he declared which were published in the New York World of March 1st, 1908, that if he does not make money out of his invention nobody else shall.

Army officers and scientific men marvelled at the great results of Bangerter's model gun.   Before the tests no one believed in its success, declaring it impossible.   Mr. Bangerter has never applied for a patent for this invention, as he intended to sell the secrets to a government, and therefore kept the plans carefully.

Naturally everyone was still skeptical as to the outcome of a standard-size gun, and to show to those who kept an eye on him that impossibilities of yesterday are made the realities of to-day, he centered his mind on another impossibility—his Perpetual Clock—while apparently forgetting his gun for a year.

"Perpetual Motion the Folly of All Ages" has become an eloquent reality.

A crowning result of his strenuous labor on this marvelous clock was the outcome of three other inventions which the studies in a large field of problems have brought to life as his anniversary self-winding clock, his fire alarm and sprinkler apparatus.   These inventions and others not here mentioned, owing to lack of space, stamp Friedrich Bangerter as a most unusual and fertile-minded inventor.

His crowning achievement in inventing that marvel of marvels—

BANGERTER'S PERPETUAL TIME CLOCK

has therefore a background of brilliant accomplishments, profound studies and many natural abilities behind a work that shall ever establish his fame as inventor of The Perpetual Clock.

BANGERTER'S AUTOMATIC JEWELER.

This Automatic Jeweler Making Collar Buttons at the Belgian
World Exposition, 1905, Often Mistaken for a Living
Man. Thousands of Collar Buttons of His Make
Were Sold Within the Exposition Grounds.

BANGERTER'S AIRSHIP, THE STAR.

Mr. Bangerter conceived the plans of his airship in 1898 and deposited the plans in France in March, 1905.

By his principles the basket, engine and traveler being about fifteen feet below the planes, it is an absolute impossibility for it to turn turtle, either by wind or storm. The four planes automatically acting as parachutes in case of descending. This airship can rise vertically and keep steady at any height, permitting the dropping of explosives with accuracy after having aimed and regulated its position.

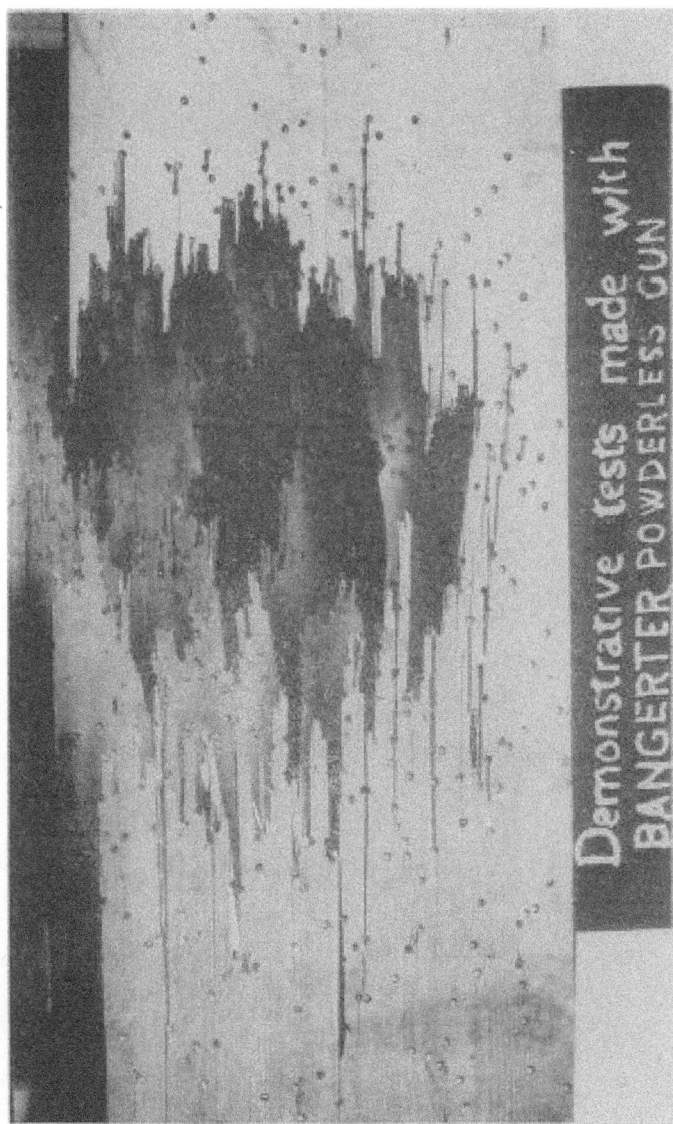

BANGERTER'S POWDERLESS GUN.

View of Targets Which Thousands of Bullets Have Pierced.
Thickness of the Targets, 2½ inch.   Time, 20 seconds.